MIDWEST SHREDS

MIDWEST SHREDS

SKATING THROUGH AMERICA'S HEARTLAND

MANDY SHUNNARAH

Belt Publishing

First Edition 2024
ISBN: 978-1-953368-71-3

Belt Publishing
5322 Fleet Avenue, Cleveland, OH 44105
www.beltpublishing.com

Book design by Jordan Koluch
Cover by David Wilson

To Jon, who kindly, gently told me I should write this book so many times that my stubborn ass started thinking it was my idea. *Midwest Shreds* wouldn't exist without your loving, prodding encouragement.

And to all the skaters from or living in the Midwest, this one's for *us*.

Table of Contents

Author's Note

In conducting interviews for this book, I sought to cast a wide net. The skaters in these pages are Black, white, Hispanic, Latinx, and Asian. They're many letters in the LGBTQ+ acronym. They are hes and shes, theydies and gentlethems. They're abled and disabled. They're plus-size and straight-size. They're amateur and pro. They're in big cities and small towns. They're skaters, skate makers, skate shop owners, and skate product creators. They skate private skate parks, city skate parks, and their own secret DIY spots. They ride skateboards, roller skates, roller blades, unicycles, and wheelchairs. Some of them have been skating for decades and others for only a year or two. Some skate competitively, others are enthusiastic hobbyists. They are, like the Midwest itself, more diverse than they get credit for.

Every single person in this book is also a better skater than I am. All of them have seen doors open through the power of rolling toys made of wood and plastic and metal on four or eight wheels.

Even as I tried to capture as many stories as possible to represent the Midwest's rich cultural history and diversity, there are many more stories I had to leave out for the sake of space. The farthest west I traveled was Des Moines and the farthest east was the Ohio-West Virginia border.

I focused on skate sports that have "skate" or "roller" in the name, like skateboarding, rollerblading, roller skating, and wheelchair skating, though BMXers and scooter riders certainly use skate parks as well. So consider this book an introductory overview rather than an exhaustive exploration. In truth, I could write ten more volumes and still not cover all of the skate magic the region has to offer.

Midwest Shreds is a look at skating in a particular time and a particular place. New skaters are born and made every day, and new parks are being built every year. Likewise, every day, someone gives up skating, and beloved skate spots are demolished or fall into disrepair. But overall, I believe the sport and its culture are evolving in a way that can permanently sustain its life. Skating isn't going anywhere in the Midwest, or anywhere else for that matter.

I started writing about skating when I couldn't physically do it, whether it was because of the weather, the coronavirus, or injuries that left me in splints and slings for weeks. For years, I've heard it said that to be a good writer, you have to write even when you're not writing. That bit of advice speaks to the fact that writing doesn't just happen when you're sitting at your computer—it happens whenever you think about writing, whenever you're processing events you might later want to write about, or whenever you're reading and contemplating the work of others.

I've found the same is true for skating. Over the last few years, during the times I was unable to lace up my skates, I found ways to skate through the subconscious act of dreaming, consciously visualizing tricks so I'd be better prepared to do them when I was at the park again. I also started cataloging some of my skating-related adventures on Instagram at @MidwestShreds, as well as sharing the many photos and videos from the road trip that made this book possible on midwestshreds.com. Go there for bonus content, photos, and videos. And feel free to share your favorite (or new) Midwest skate spots.

Of course, even during those times where I couldn't skate myself, I was writing about it, and as you read through these pages, as you meet the wide variety of people who make up skate culture in the Midwest, I hope you'll also hear the crunching scrape of small, hard wheels and feel a breeze of your own creation.

Introduction

If I were to ask you to think of skaters and skate parks, I assume a couple of things might pop in your head: Tony Hawk and his eponymous *Pro Skater* video game, skating in empty pools, Dogtown and Z-Boys, and, of course, California.

Let's be honest, you probably weren't thinking about the Midwest. Admittedly, I didn't either until I moved here. But when you look closer, the region has a long, storied history in skating of all types—roller skating, roller blading, and skateboarding—and without the Midwest, these sports wouldn't have been popularized at the rate they were, nor would they be in the zeitgeist to the degree they are today. While California and the West Coast might be thought of as skate havens, the Midwest has undeniably impacted the trajectory of skating in its many forms for nearly two hundred years.

And yet when skating—particularly skateboarding and the culture around skating ramps—is mentioned, it's often California and the West Coast that first come to mind. This is due to one simple reason: While midwesterners were designing, patenting, and manufacturing skates, Californians were pushing the limits of what could be done on them. They weren't skating outside merely to get from one place to another or to take a rolling stroll through the park. They were turning skating into an action sport, the likes of which the world had never seen before.

———

The first roller skates were invented by an enterprising theater company that wanted to mimic ice skating in a stage production, and by the 1850s, roller skating had become popular enough that dedicated roller rinks were being opened in England. However, those early inlines didn't allow for much more than going in a straight line or turning in a wide berth, so it wasn't until the creation of the "turning roller skate," the quads most common at rinks now, that roller skating really took off.

By the 1880s, rinks dotted the United States, and roller skates were being mass-produced by Micajah C. Henley, a Richmond, Indiana, man dubbed the "king of roller skates." Working from the expired patent of Massachusetts-born James Leonard Plimpton's 1863 quad roller skate, Henley added ball bearings for speed and toe stops for brakes to improve upon the design. Henley Roller Skate Works began in a stable at the back of his parents' property and, after expanding five times to accommodate demand and hiring more employees beyond his five sisters, Henley had a two-story factory built in downtown Richmond.

Though Richmond, Indiana, abuts the Ohio state line and is more than 250 miles away from the Second City, Henley named his bestselling skate the Chicago Skate. At the height of his factory's success, three hundred employees were making two thousand pairs of Chicago Skates every day to be sold around the world. Though Henley died in 1927, his son, brother-in-law, and nephew kept the company running until the start of World War II, a time in which no roller skates were manufactured in the US because they weren't essential for the war effort.

Despite the similarity in their name, Henley's Chicago Skates had little to do with the Chicago Roller Skate Company, which was founded in 1905 by two brothers, Ralph and Walter Ware, who were actually based in the Windy City. Another brother, Robert, joined the company in 1907, and by 1910, there were thirty-five employees manufacturing skates in a factory on Washington Boulevard.

During World War I, the Chicago Roller Skate Company took a break from skate-making to lend their equipment to the war effort. A year later, however, the company's output grew so much that they had to relocate to an even larger factory space. This growth bolstered the company through the darkest times of the Depression and allowed them to remain in business.

As the love of roller skating continued to grow around the country, the demand for skates that could withstand the rigors of the outdoors grew too. The Chicago Roller Skate Company was the first to manufacture wheels designed specifically for outdoor rolling. Indoor wheels at the time were made of steel, so the company affixed rubber tires around the steel wheels, mimicking automobiles.

After the company's skate manufacturing hiatus during World War II, the business continued to grow, eventually producing 3,250 pairs of skates each day. What helped ensure the Chicago Roller Skate Company's success is that in addition to assembling the skates, they manufactured nearly all of the hardware the skates required in-house. And the company's ability to produce its own hardware—as well as customize hardware for specific needs—allowed it to play a formative role in the invention of the skateboard in the 1960s.

Before the folks at Val Surf, a family-owned surfboard shop in Los Angeles, reached out to the Chicago Roller Skate Company for standardized parts to build better skateboards in 1962, the "sidewalk surfers" of the day bought old roller skates from rinks, disassembled them, and attached the parts to planks of wood. The Chicago Roller Skate Company sold the parts, though it wasn't keen on the idea of skateboarding itself, believing it was a passing fad, and they didn't make inroads to capture that segment of the market. Though many of the early skateboard manufacturers went belly-up, ultimately, Chicago's reluctance to embrace skateboarding (and later, inline skates) quickened the company's demise.

The Chicago Roller Skate Company's second generation of family business owners included Gordon Ware, who made one of the earliest designs for inline skates in 1966. Inline skating hadn't caught on by then, especially with the disco era just around the corner, so the design was shelved. In 1981, believing that inline skates would never take off, Chicago Roller Skate Company executives sold their inline patent to Scott Olson, a teenager from Minneapolis who wanted to play hockey outside in the warmer months. Olson would go on to create Rollerblade, a product now so synonymous with inline skating that "rollerblading" is used to mean just that. While Rollerblade would go on to become a multimillion-dollar company, the Chicago Roller Skate Company would be sold and dissolved into another sporting goods company in the 1990s, thus ending its ninety-year reign.

———————

While both skate manufacturing and skate tricks are important, the latter makes for a flashier visual image, as indicated in the numerous skate photography magazines and clip videos that have proliferated over the past sixty years. The first skateboard magazine, called the *Quarterly Skateboarder*, was published in 1964 out of California, as nearly all the earliest skate magazines were. As it transitioned into a bimonthly called simply *Skateboarder*, more publications followed in its wake, the most popular being *Thrasher*, which was first published in 1981 out of San Francisco, and *Transworld Skateboarding*, which launched in 1983 out of Carlsbad, California.

The first skate video—*Skaterdater*, which was filmed in 1965—also came from California. Almost two decades later, *The Bones Brigade*

Video Show, filmed throughout Southern California, became one of the first films made to highlight skaters' tricks. The video's release in 1984 coincided with the rising popularity of VCRs, so while *The Bones Brigade Video Show* was only expected to sell three hundred copies, it ended up selling thirty thousand. The video featured a young Tony Hawk, helping propel his rise to fame.

Following the demand for VCRs, camcorders released in the early 1980s allowed for the kind of ease of use and portability that pushed video cameras—and their subjects—into the mainstream. With the introduction of the camcorder in 1980, recording video was no longer reserved for professional filmmakers or those wealthy enough to afford the equipment. An ESPN documentary on the history of skate videos notes that at this time, when consumer video cameras were in their earliest stages, skateboarding wasn't on TV often. The simultaneous rise in the popularity of both homemade videos and skateboarding helped make the sport more accessible and quicken its spread.

While there was certainly skate media coming out of the Midwest in the 1980s and 1990s, it came after the initial wave out of California, which set the tone and aesthetic for what viewers should expect from skate media. This included the use of the wide-angle, fisheye lens and bright, bold colors. Because early camcorders tended to mute colors, skaters wore high-contrast clothes so they stood out against the background, giving them a vibrant, larger-than-life effect.

Despite the Midwest playing a massive role in the history of skating, the lack of compelling visual imagery that captured the public's attention from those early days of the sport has maligned the region in many skaters' minds. Some even believe, falsely, that no one skates here even today.

Skaters, by and large, seemed to have no idea about the region's hidden gems. I came across the message boards for *Slap Magazine*, a skateboard magazine that began in 1992. While the magazine went out of print in 2008 and doesn't currently post editorial content online, the magazine's message boards are an active hub of skate news and rumors, with hundreds of users logging on every day.

Here's a post from June 2019:

Topic: What place/country would you like to visit?

Bumpovertrash: Anywhere in europe, japan china australia fuckin anywhere but midwest america

And from May 2020:

Topic: What brands will you never buy?

Willie: SHAKE JUNT and Grizzly Grip. I could see having to hold my nose and buying some dumb shit if was stuck in a foreign country or small town in the midwest but if I have to look down and see either of those, it ain't worth it.

Saint Coke: what's wrong with the midwest? I live there and we have all the same stuff you have.

I could go on. The message boards have over a decade's worth of archives—thousands of pages on every topic imaginable, including ripping on the Midwest, as long as it's at least tangentially related to skateboarding.

Though skateboarding may have originated in southern California when surfers wanted a comparable activity to do when the waves were flat, that doesn't entirely explain the entrenchment of "skate culture = West Coast" in our collective imagination. After all, Mardi Gras was first celebrated in Mobile, Alabama, but the first place that comes to mind when you hear about it will forever be New Orleans.

If you view skating by who's on TV or who gets endorsement deals, it would be easy to get the impression that the coasts dominate the skating world. There are seventy-eight professional skateboarders with Wikipedia pages, and twenty-nine grew up in California. Another ten were born or mostly skated in the Northeast. Meanwhile, just twelve are from the Midwest, Rust Belt, and Appalachia. But that doesn't give a full picture of the sport, especially considering how relatively new it is. Skateboarding was a fringe sport until recently, and aggressive inline and quad skating have produced few celebrities or professionals. The vast majority of roller-skating and rollerblading celebrities who are well-known to those of us deeply entrenched in this world (but largely unknown outside of it) don't have Wikipedia pages.

Perhaps a more accurate way to get a sense of skate culture is to look at the number of skate parks per capita in a state or geographic region. After all, building a skate park is a huge and expensive endeavor; it requires a fairly large amount of space and thousands or tens of thousands of dollars in materials. It's not a project a city would undertake lightly if there was little demand.

A look at Google Maps tells me there are 224 skate parks in California—unsurprising for a state that takes up at least three-quarters of the US's western seaboard and the state that invented skateboarding. That means there's a skate park for roughly every 176,000 people. That sounds like a lot until you do the same math for Pennsylvania, which has 147 skate parks, or one for roughly every 87,000 people. Similarly, Ohio has 123 skate parks, which is one for roughly every 95,000 people. Together, Pennsylvania and Ohio have more skate parks and far more skate parks per capita than California, despite having less than half the population.

Of course, Google Maps is not the ultimate authority on hubs of skate culture. In addition to what Google Maps shows, there are also untold numbers of DIY spaces—like ramps in the garage, a grind rail in the backyard, or a whole half-pipe if someone has the space and the will to fight the weather to maintain it. So in reality, the skate park to skater ratio is even lower than any official count.

And, as one friend asked when I told her about this book, "Aren't all the California skaters just skating empty pools?"

Perhaps. Nonetheless, all these skate parks in the Rust Belt wouldn't exist if there weren't skaters to shred them. This raises the ultimate question of this book: When will midwestern and Rust Belt skaters get their due?

———————

All of this is what led me, a twenty-eight-year-old, plus-size, and otherwise nonathletic person in Columbus, Ohio, to fulfill a childhood dream to lace up my quads and shred 'til I'm dead.

There are dozens of different kinds of skating. There are subcategories of skateboarding, like street skating and longboarding, in addition to park skating. There are factions of rollerbladers who do slalom, off-road, and artistic skating as well, on top of aggressive inline skating. Roller skating includes speed skating and artistic skating, which is more like traditional figure skating on ice, in addition to aggressive park skating. There is a long history of rink roller skating, jam skating, and dance skating, primarily done by the Black community, the same community who is tirelessly fighting against rink closures around the country. Likewise, there is a history of roller derby throughout the Midwest and the Rust Belt, and its history is best told by the athletes who have helped mold it into the sport we know it as today. (I recommend *Collective Chaos: A Roller Derby Team Memoir* by Samantha Tucker and Amy Spears for that particular historical account.)

Additionally, although BMXers enjoy the same ramps as skaters, there is nuance to their history that is best told by cyclists—or at least someone who isn't terrified of flipping over the handlebars on flat ground. The same is true for those who ride scooters, as well as the countless other devices people use to shred skate parks. If you can attach wheels to a nonmotorized device, someone is riding it at a skate park. My focus here is on the people who call what they do "skating"—whether that's skateboarding, roller skating, inline skating, or WCMX, also known as wheelchair motocross and chairskating.

For the purposes of this book, I'm only concerned with the type of skating that's done at skate parks—on ramps, rails, blocks, banks, and the like—specifically within the Rust Belt and where the Rust Belt bleeds into Appalachia and the Midwest at large. Because the borders of these regions are inexact at best and there is undoubtedly some overlap, I've chosen to take a broad approach when it comes to location.

Aggressive park skating is as much of a lifestyle as it is a sport. Skate culture has influenced music, fashion, and writing, primarily through indie bands, indie brands, and indie zines. And though Midwest skaters have been overshadowed by their West Coast compatriots, Rust Belt skate culture evolved apart from West Coast skate culture and is its own separate entity. Despite being historically underrepresented in the skate world, Rust Belt skaters continue to thrive, and our numbers continue to grow. Midwestern skaters are laying claim to their history and reinventing the wheely sports they love in the region where they feel at home. I know because I've seen it happen.

Even so, *Midwest Shreds* is less of a corrective history and more of a look at our current cultural moment, while attempting to give long overdue credit to everything that was involved in getting to this point. In West Lafayette, Indiana, I talked to a born-and-bred Hoosier who built the skate park of his dreams in his own backyard, creating a rollerblade haven, because growing up, the closest skate parks to him were four to five hours away. In St. Louis, I saw how a skate park breathed new life into a formerly abandoned cathedral built in 1886 and how racism rears its ugly head in skating in a place so close to where Michael Brown was murdered. In Des Moines, I went to a brand-new, freshly cemented skate park that, with its opening, became the largest in the country, as well as being the host of the only Olympic-qualifying event in North America for skateboarding's inauguration to the Olympics in 2020. These are just three of the many iconic and underground skate spots featured in this book.

The chapters follow my road trip map, starting in and around Columbus, then moving clockwise through the region and back to the beginning. I collected far more stories than I was able to use in the book, but they all speak to a gritty Midwest DIY ethos and an insatiable love of all things skating in this region. Though the West Coast might have skate parks galore, they don't have *these* skate parks. And writing this book has clearly shown me what a lot of skaters choose to ignore: it's fucking rad here in the Midwest.

In another post from the *Slap* message boards, this one dated January 2014, a young guy living with his parents in a small town in the Midwest was ranting about how he couldn't wait to escape.

In reply:

paraquat: typical young person Midwest attitude. Hating where you are and thinking big cities are superior. While big cities are epicenters for culture, a small city can offer some refreshing aspects . . . keep in mind that happiness is not necessarily waiting for you in Colorado or California.

pencil: i never understood the midwest hate, i fucking loved every minute i lived in cincinnati but all anyone talked about was "WHEN I GRADUATE IM GOIN TO CALI TO SMOKE MAD WEED BRA." Like wtf, living in the midwest is not a prison sentence, it's the god damn best thing in the world!

It's one thing to want to see what the rest of the world has to offer, but to write off an entire region, especially one that has commendable amenities for the lifestyle sport you want to practice, seems like cutting off your nose to spite your face. If I hadn't moved to the Midwest, I wouldn't have become the skater I'd dreamed of being since I was a little kid watching *Brink!* on the Disney Channel. The movie is a modern retelling—or at least "modern" in 1998 when the movie was released—of *Hans Brinker, or The Silver Skates* by Mary Mapes Dodge, which was originally published in 1865. The protagonist, Brink, and his skate crew, the Soul Skaters, skate for the love of aggressive inline and frequently clash with the local professional blade team in town. The plot is secondary to the skate scenes featuring big ramps and bigger air. When I returned from my road trip, I watched the movie again, my first viewing as an adult. This time, I paid less attention to the specific tricks the bladers were doing and more to the skate parks themselves. Instead of yearning to go there, this time I thought, *Eh, I've skated better.* The fact is that if you can't find places to skate in the Midwest, you're either not looking hard enough or you're lacking imagination.

While I'm convinced skating in the Midwest is "the god damn best thing in the world," that isn't the case for everybody. And I'd be remiss if I didn't mention the overwhelming whiteness of skate media, both historically and in the present-day, and both on the West Coast and in the Midwest.

Though there are more BIPOC professional skaters, skate brand owners, and skate media owners today, there are still many magazine spreads and videos that would have you believe there are few Black and Brown skaters. In the days before skate parks were normalized and built regularly (if not often enough), this might have been true. Before skate parks, street skating and aggressive skating would have taken place either on private property, with or without permission, and in public spaces where nonskaters might create a hostile environment for skaters and make them feel unwelcome. Despite the lack of official data on the subject, I can only imagine how often business owners called the cops on Black and Brown youth for skating in their parking lots and plazas.

And as we know, run-ins with the police can be deadly for Black and Brown people.

The stereotype of skaters facing hostility from cops is founded in truth—without a dedicated place to skate, skaters are forced into spaces where they're more likely to be under police surveillance in a way that other sports are not. Football fields, baseball fields, soccer fields, tennis courts, and basketball courts are all dedicated spaces for their respective sports, and if someone is practicing that sport in its dedicated space, they're less likely to be accosted by police.

However, this stereotype of police harassing skaters has led to the widespread—and false—belief that all skaters are juvenile delinquents, and the proliferation of this stereotype has at times made skating a deadly sport for BIPOC, especially Black folks. Camrin William De'Ron Starr was shot and killed while riding a skateboard in Cincinnati in 2015; his murder remains unsolved. Though some treat skating like it's a sport set apart from society at large with an us-versus-them, authentic-skaters-against-posers-and-normies attitude, in reality, all the same issues that exist in larger society—including racism—also exist in skating.

There are other stereotypes about skaters to contend with, too, namely that of the slacker stoner. While cannabis is used within and outside of the skate community, the fact remains that skating in all its forms requires great focus, dedication, and perseverance to get good. "Slacking" and skating are incongruent with one another. It's that very dedication to the sport that makes skateboarding, rollerblading, aggressive quad skating, and wheelchair skating more than fun hobbies and clip videos on social media reduced to a handful of cool tricks.

While I can't speak to the skate communities on the West Coast, in my own experience, I know the skate community in the Midwest and Rust Belt to be expansive, diverse, and welcoming. I can't help thinking that skaters must rally together even more to form strong, dedicated communities in parts of the country where we tend to be underrepresented by skate media at large. In researching and writing *Midwest Shreds*, I got to witness firsthand the strength of midwestern skate communities. My hope is that this book and other rising Midwest-centric skate media will finally give the region's skaters their due.

WORTHINGTON SKATE PARK

A t 10:00 a.m. on a Wednesday, I didn't expect to find Worthington Skate Park crowded, and I wasn't disappointed. Other than the few joggers on the nearby bike trail along the Olentangy River in this suburb of Columbus, I was the only person there.

I checked the weather in advance and knew it would be a sunny, reasonably warm day in April, unplagued by spring rain. I took the day off work, even going as far as to let my coworkers know what I was doing, and they eagerly awaited pics and videos.

So it was that on April 3, 2019, I started aggressive quad skating—though on my Bambi legs, my teetering around on wheels didn't feel "aggressive" at all.

I'd purchased my park-ready quads—so different from the lightweight rink skates I was used to—with their sturdy, ankle-high boots, gummy wheels that could smoothly roll over uneven concrete terrain, and hefty slabs of metal connecting the wheels to the boot, in anticipation of this moment. If I'm being honest, I also purchased them for their style: a peach boot with glittery lavender wheels and matching laces. Together, at seven pounds, they are the world's most beautiful ankle weights.

I was twenty-eight at the time, and some might think I was a little old to be learning how to shred. After all, isn't park skating for kids and teenagers with pliable bones and a lack of frontal lobe development that allows for questionable decision-making? What makes a reasonable adult strap wheels to her feet and jump off the top of a curved piece of concrete where she might *literally* break her face at the bottom?

I grew up in the small towns north of Birmingham, Alabama. Today, the state has thirty-five skate parks, though in the 1990s and early 2000s, none of them were close to me. But what I did have access to was a skating rink.

It was inevitable that I'd learn how to skate. Between the field trips and birthday parties and church outings to Funtime Skate Center, it seemed like I was there all the time. Both the elementary school I went to and my best friend's church also had rooms attached to their basketball courts where there were shelves of standard rent-a-skates. In middle school, I marked time by counting down until the next Friday night, when the coupon printed on that week's school lunch menu would get me half off admission. I was skating all the time—it was just always indoors on a smooth, flat surface.

It didn't occur to me that skating on elevated surfaces was something I'd like to do until *Viva La Bam* aired on MTV in 2003, the same year I became a latchkey kid. The show chronicled the adventures of professional skateboarder and former *Jackass* stuntman Bam Margera. My young teenage self didn't realize that the show's drama—which usually revolved around a challenge Bam had to solve through skateboarding or pranks— was clearly manufactured for TV, and I found Bam's life glamorous. A professional skateboarder! The novelty!

I dreamed about becoming a pro skateboarder too, minus the pranks. I'd call myself Bang Matranga, and my logo would be the anarchy symbol turned into a heart. Very original.

With about thirty-five dollars in allowance money, I bought my first skateboard on a family Walmart run. The idea of a dedicated skate shop felt foreign in rural Alabama; Walmart and K-Mart were the only places nearby where it was even possible to get a board. Even the PacSun store at the mall, which sold skate-related clothing, didn't sell skateboards or anything you'd need to maintain one. Mostly, kids went there to get puffy DC Shoes—or in my case, black and hot pink Etnies. Walmart's options were slim: I could get a skateboard with a handlebar attachment, clearly intended for young children, or I could get the adult-looking skateboard with the black deck and red wheels.

I took my red-wheeled skateboard out into the driveway, trying to remember the moves I'd seen Bam do. This was before the advent of YouTube, so searching for how-to skate videos on the internet wasn't an option. Sitting with my face mere inches from the TV, meticulously studying Bam's tricks in hopes of replicating them was the only thing I could do.

Step onto the board, toes pointed perpendicular to the length of the deck. Bend your knees. The deeper the bend, the faster you go; the straighter you stand, the higher your center of gravity and the poorer your balance. Use your back foot to push yourself and gain momentum. Lean to turn slowly. Lean back, lifting the front wheels off the ground and throwing your upper body in the direction you want to go to make a fast turn. Shift your weight backward, jump, then quickly shift your weight forward for an ollie. Do that with one foot on the edge of the board, kicking the deck into a spin, for a kickflip. Soon, the rhythms of balance and shifting my weight became more natural. The glossary of tricks became a part of my body's vocabulary.

When my mother told me there were no skate parks near our house, I didn't believe her. I asked the skater kids at school and they demurred. Since we weren't allowed to bring our skateboards to school, none of us had actually seen one another skate. We'd meet up on Mondays and describe epic tricks we'd done in half-pipes over the weekend, breaking our expensive, brand-name boards and having to go several towns away to buy another one. We were lying, of course. Limited by our resources—we were just barely middle-class, if that—and all of us living several dozen miles from the nearest half-pipe, we were all making up stories of what we *hoped* we'd do if we had a skate park. What we imagined we'd be doing if we had more than a curb, a piece of plywood on a staircase, and a sloped driveway. We dressed in T-shirts with brand logos, we wore the wide, padded shoes of skateboarders, and we listened to punk music, but deep inside, we were our worst fear, that which we accused everyone else of being and hoped to never be ourselves: poseurs.

We were all just latchkey kids who watched *Viva La Bam* and longed for a life we couldn't, in practicality, have or afford. So we did the best we could with our scene-kid clothes, our screamo music, and our Walmart boards. Some might say that donning the effects of skaters does not a skater make, but what is a skateboarder if not an innovator who once bolted wheels to the bottom of a wood crate and called it sidewalk surfing? What is "authentic" skate culture if not scrappy, improvisational DIY in all respects?

With the confirmation that I was "shit out of luck, dude" for a skate park, I contented myself with the streets. Or rather, the one street I lived on. Ridgeland Drive was shaped like a barbell, with cul-de-sacs on either end and two connecting streets in the middle. It was technically in a subdivision, something that felt like the antithesis of the skate aesthetic, but I had to make do.

Our street had an incline that felt minuscule if you were walking or in a car, but with four small wheels under your feet, it could fling you headlong downward at a rapid clip. I'd managed to make it down small sections of the street without killing myself, so one day, I steeled my courage. My mother was out working in the garden, and I wanted to prove to her that this hobby of mine was not a waste of time and that I could be a real skater even without access to a skate park. I started at the very top of the hill, the first time I'd done so, and planned—prayed—to make it to the bottom.

The ride wasn't unlike the drop of a roller coaster—slow at first, then quickly gaining momentum. The hill was too steep, and I was going too fast to be able to carve side to side, mitigating my speed. I slipped off the board, falling forward, tumbling down the hill without a helmet. I rolled to a stop on my bruised and bloodied hands and knees, just in time to see my skateboard roll straight into the storm drain, the splash echoing from its depths below.

Open-mouthed, I ran to the curb and knelt beside the hole. My mother's bellowing laugh pierced the air between us. As if the loss of my skateboard in such a ridiculous manner wasn't insulting enough, the storm drain that had swallowed it was right in front of my house. I lay in the gutter and thrust my arm inside, trying to get a sense of how deep the drain was. My mother's hand yanked the scruff of my shirt.

"Get outta there! You'll get bit by a water moccasin!" she hollered between gasping laughs.

I was too flabbergasted to say anything. As rickety and cheap as it was, I loved that skateboard and couldn't bear the thought of using my hard-earned allowance to buy things that were liable to get eaten by storm drains. I only had the one street to skate on given my mother's overprotectiveness, and its half dozen storm drains weren't going anywhere. As a result, roller skating became the safer bet. You'd be hard-pressed to lose something attached to your feet.

You might be wondering why, since I already knew how to roller skate, I didn't try roller skating outside. The answer is simple: I'd never seen anyone do it before, so I didn't conceive of it as a possibility. It's hard to be what you can't see. And because I thought skating only happened indoors on rented skates at rinks and church basketball courts, I didn't even own a pair myself until much later.

Years after this, I moved with my partner to Columbus, Ohio, and had all but forgotten about skating. I'd gone to college in Birmingham, not far from where I grew up, so living in a place that lacked a skate park was a problem that persisted into my adult life. I'd reconciled that it just wasn't meant to be. I, too, bought into the misconception that everywhere but the coasts was as devoid of skate parks as my Alabama hometown.

We bought a house in 2017, paying no mind to the fact that it was a mere five-minute drive from an indoor roller rink. At the time, the house's bigger selling point was the built-in bookshelf upstairs and the Half Price Books across the road. But toward the end of 2018, some friends invited me to join them for adult night at Skate Zone 71, so named for the nearby interstate. At that point, I was twenty-eight and hadn't skated in well over a decade.

Muscle memory is a beautiful thing. From the moment I stepped onto the gleaming floor at Skate Zone 71, it was like I'd never left. I could still skate just as well as I had in middle school, at the peak of my zooming around the rink at top speed. "Bounce, Rock, Skate, Roll," the classic skate song, pumped through the speakers, and I adjusted my rhythm to match the beat. As the night progressed, more people arrived, and the music turned to current hits and rap from the nineties. What started out as twenty-five or so people at 9:00 p.m. turned into well over one hundred by midnight. Most of the people there were serious skaters, breakdancing on skates, doing entire couples dance routines on skates, doing dozens of spins at a time, footwork so smooth it would have been impressive for any regular-shoed dancer, and jumping into double axels like they were weightless—all moves contributed to rink skating by the Black community.

I continued going to adult night skates nearly every Thursday and Sunday after that, the two weekly time slots when Skate Zone 71 wasn't overrun with tottering small children. Throughout the winter, I punctuated my weeks with eager trips to the rink. And when the next spring came, I felt confident enough to look for skate parks around town.

Worthington Skate Park, which is about a fifteen-minute drive north of downtown Columbus, isn't the best skate park in the world, though it was the first one I'd ever been to, so I didn't know that at the time. At first, I was intimidated by its six-foot ramps, the angles of its banks, and *all* that concrete. It wasn't the smooth concrete I'd hoped for, but the kind with small rocks throughout—perfect for ripping skin to confetti upon the slightest contact. Because I was twenty-eight and old enough to know better, I came suited up in a helmet, knee pads, elbow pads, and wrist guards.

This time, I'd prepared with YouTube videos. Stagger your feet. Bend your knees. Lean forward. Keep your eyes where you want to go, and keep them off your feet unless you want to end up on the ground. Stagger. Bend. Lean. Stagger. Bend. Lean.

I stood at the top of a four-foot bank, a platform with an incline like a wheelchair ramp or a narrow wedge of cheese. I visualized myself going down and safely making it to the bottom. I pep-talked myself, first in my head, then aloud. No one else was around to hear me or talk me out of this.

"Stagger, bend, lean. Stagger bend lean. *Staggerbendlean!*"

For a moment, I felt weightless, like I'd broken a law of nature, gracefully losing altitude. Almost as quickly as my adrenaline kicked in, I was on the ground, still rolling, still upright. I realized, *I'm in control!* And it's not an exaggeration to say it was as if the world had revealed a secret to me.

I came to a stop, not because I was worried about crashing but because I was smiling so wide my cheeks hurt. My heart pummeled inside my chest, not from exertion—after all, gravity did most of the work—but because I was so naturally high on the feeling.

I've heard it said that walking is a controlled fall. You can think of skating, then, as controlled soaring. To skate a ramp is to fly without wings.

And after that first time in Worthington, I couldn't wait to do it again.

Columbus, Ohio

SKATE NAKED

The sound is something like a scrape, maybe from a rough-grain sandpaper. At first you can't help noticing how loud it is—how loud *you* are—riding with these four or eight wheels on the concrete. The sound of the rolling wheels is almost frenetic, and you feel frenzied. What is skating if not an attempt to escape something, even if it's yourself? Even going in circles or back and forth on a ramp is still putting distance between you and whatever drove you to the skate park in the first place.

Eventually, you stop noticing the scraping sound because it's always there, like the hum of a city at night—a throbbing that's proof of life. And like the heartbeat of a city, you come to only notice it when it's not there. I live in Columbus, Ohio, a city with one indoor skate park. In winter, and when the outdoor parks have ice frozen in the bottom of their bowls and snow coating the banks and the tops of their rails, the indoor park, Skate Naked, becomes a crowded place.

There's a camaraderie among those of us who are willing to leave our warm homes in the cold to drive to this chilly warehouse in the no-man's-land near the airport to skate in the dead of winter, when some days, it's already dark by the time Skate Naked opens at 3:00 p.m. We're all itching to put wheels under our fragile bodies, which we've convinced ourselves against better judgment aren't so fragile after all.

Aside from the pejorative "flyover country," which is a term aimed more at the rural parts of the Midwest, cities in the region seem to exist in the popular imagination as islands of decay. It's a place rife with the skeletons of former factories, the husks of great industry packed up and gone away. People outside the Midwest see the curated tragedy porn on the news and see misfortune, sadness, defeat. They don't see what we see: possibility. From the outside, Skate Naked is a nondescript building. Its many bay doors, high ceilings, and cinder block walls indicate the businesses that were here before involved shipping with eighteen-wheelers. The floors that were first made smooth for forklifts now give skaters their speed, enough to feel the force of the air push their hair back when they drop precipitously off the larger ramps.

Jeff Trasin and Jon Hammond, the owners of Skate Naked, had the vision to see what the old warehouse could be, an indoor skate park the city so desperately needed. What was first the Buckeye Potato Chip plant in the 1950s, then later a golf cart showroom and then a window and siding shop, was transformed by their hands.

"When we first saw it, it was empty. Nobody else would've looked at this place and thought it was awesome," Jon said, speaking of his gut feeling that this was where they should be.

"I was like, we can do this, we just need to paint it," Jeff added, laughing, knowing there was so much more work ahead of them than that.

On the whole, midwesterners are practical people, dedicated to function and resourcefulness. Aesthetics are secondary, and in Skate Naked's case, they're hardly considered at all. With the exception of a spray-painted mural above the big bowl, the park is gritty, both in the literal and figurative sense. The walls are painted black, and in some places, they're built from black painted plywood. On one particular roll-in, you're liable to get a splinter if you fall. The roof above both bowls leaks, and you have to carve fast on your feet to avoid wiping out on a rainy day. The sheets of coating over the wood ramps are often flaking, and woe be unto you if you're the unlucky soul whose wheels add just the right amount of pressure to break through to the other side. I'm always surprised by the creative places patrons find to make DIY trash cans—behind a ramp, inside a wall where a piece of plywood has come loose, or just the edges of any old platform—and I never leave without a deep coating of black grime under my fingernails.

And I love it. There's no place I'd rather be.

Skate Naked feels like home in the way that only a place abundant with memories can. It's where I learned to drop in properly on a ramp, where I learned to pump a half-pipe, where I learned to jump stairs, where I learned to one-eighty over a bank, and where I made my first skate friends. And it is the place where, eventually, one day, if I don't die trying, I'll drop into the big bowl and get a couple of good carves in before losing momentum. For me, Skate Naked carries an air of nostalgia, even as it's thriving and more skaters are choosing it as their home skate park.

"We wanted to make a good spot for kids, and as long as it's kid-friendly, everyone else will come. The original guy who ran it before we took over wanted skateboards only, and it was like, no, we have to open this thing up to everybody," Jon said. "Ten years ago, we didn't get any girl skaters. Now we've got so many girls, even little girls coming to the lessons on Saturdays. Before, it was such a closed community, and now it's wide open."

The winter of 2020 and 2021 was an especially brutal one. While Columbus's winters tend to be mild, there was about a three-week period when temperatures didn't get above freezing, so the snow never melted. And when it finally warmed up, it did so only marginally. The streets and outdoor skate parks turned into a slippery slush that was treacherous even to walk on. But through it all, Skate Naked was there—a beacon—as long as you weren't too afraid of the coronavirus.

I'm thirty-two now, which is still young enough to quiet the voice in my head that tells me I'm going to break every bone in my face if I fall off a six-foot ramp or crash into a rail. But thirty-two also means I'm old enough to be cognizant of my own mortality and fear of being intubated just because I wanted so badly to skate at the only indoor skate park that I would put myself in a spot where the 'rona was likely to take up residence in my lungs.

I hardly skated at all that winter, and my body ached with longing for the ramps' changing elevation. Nearly every night, I dreamed about skating, nailing tricks I'd never done in real life and getting the kind of air that's only possible in the imagination (unless your name is Tony Hawk). Even in my sleep, I could feel the texture of the ramp, the heart-dropping-into-the-stomach sensation of flinging myself down its slope. In my dreams, the panic that hits the moment when you know you're going to crash was gone, as was the pain of feeling the wind knocked out of me. In the morning, I'd wake to search for the bruises I wear like badges, trophies, battle scars, the bruises that purpled my shins, thighs, elbows, and especially my ass, where there was, more often than not, the imprinted kiss of a skate wheel, sometimes deep enough to qualify as a hematoma.

Skating requires fearlessness, which is the antithesis of who I am and thus what I long to be. I'm afraid of everything and have the anxiety medication to prove it. But on the other side of fear is curiosity, and more than anything, I'm curious about skating. Curious enough to hear the voice in my head, the one that says, *You're going to fall and grind your teeth down on the concrete until you have nothing but little nubs and raw nerves left, and you'll hit with such force that you pass out cold, and when you awake, you'll have found you pissed yourself, and the ambulance ride is going to bankrupt you,* and tell it to shut the fuck up.

The question of why, when I am afraid of so much, I would choose this action sport, is simple. Skating is the only sport I remain curious about in a healthy way. I tried running and became so obsessed with miles run, my speed, and the calories I burned that I gave myself an eating disorder. I tried spin classes and pushed my body nearly to passing out just to stay at the top of the leaderboard. I tried yoga and became so driven in the pursuit of a lithe, slender "yoga body" that I relapsed into my eating disorder. I tried push-ups and sit-ups and free weights, counting reps into the hundreds. In between these periods, I would swear off exercise entirely. I am the workout equivalent of an alcoholic—I cannot have just one sip, just one drink. If I partake, it is wholeheartedly, even to my own detriment.

The skate park, though, is not given to measurement. There are no reps to be counted, no miles to be logged, and no leaderboard to be topped. When I skate, I'm so focused on the next step, the next move, the next obstacle ahead of me—simply not dying—that I cannot possibly divide my brain into the components required to constantly assess myself.

Skating is inherently rebellious. It's against authority because we say fuck private property and skate there anyway. It's against infrastructure because if you don't build us a skate park, we'll make our own and terrorize the sidewalks in the meantime. It's against corporate sensibilities because indie brands—whether it's clothing, shoes, or the wheels themselves—rule the scene. It's against convention and sometimes even against society at large because even though skating has its communities, it is notably not a team sport. Skating is my way of rebelling against diet culture, against #thinspiration, and against whatever the latest shame-based weight-loss cult du jour says. It's the only way I've found to move my body in a way that doesn't push me somewhere I don't need to go.

I don't know that I would have discovered my love of skate parks if I lived anywhere outside the Midwest, and Columbus in particular. You can be a beginner here. Columbus is constantly reinventing itself, and over the last few decades, it has gone from farm town to corporate business haven to one of the fastest growing cities in the country. It's a city beloved by people as disparate as Arnold Schwarzenegger, Saeed Jones, and the late Aaron Carter—none of whom are from here originally but who all have made the city a second home.

I've talked to skaters outside the Midwest, and several have mentioned that there's a pressure at some skate parks to know what you're doing or to at least have the decency to get out of the way of the people who do. There's no patience for beginners, especially not beginner adults. But I've never sensed that here. Nearly anywhere you are within the Columbus metro area, you're within spitting distance of a skate park. Some are large, some are small, but there are enough of them that, with the exception of Skate Naked in winter or on rainy summer days, they rarely get too crowded. A more spread-out population of skaters means you're rarely competing for space, so there's little pressure to get out of the bowl quickly if you're still trying to learn how the curves flow. There's little pressure to get off the top of a ramp if you need a minute to talk yourself into stepping over the coping and letting its slope propel you through your fear.

With skate parks in so many of its neighborhoods, I could be a beginner in Columbus. I could roll, fall, collect my bruises like Girl Scout patches, get up, and do it all again with minimal dirty looks. Skate Naked and the other parks of Columbus allowed me to learn. I skate because I live here. I live here because I can skate here.

West Lafayette, Indiana

SCHMIDTY'S RAMP & CAMP

chmidty's is the kind of place I felt like I should whisper about. The address isn't posted online anywhere, and if you search for Schmidty's on Google Maps, you'll end up at a gas station in rural Ohio, in the exact opposite direction of where you need to be. Not that Google Maps would help you. You'd be better off getting the exact coordinates from a skater in the know.

It was my first time going to the rollerblade haven that is Schmidty's, and after winding around the looping roads outside of the Purdue University campus, I saw a sign spray-painted with "R&C" and an arrow. Turning onto the dirt driveway, I saw a wide grassy field ahead packed full of cars, tents, and firepits.

Ramp & Camp is exactly what it sounds like: a place where one comes to skate ramps and camp on the property. Both ramp and camp areas border a tranquil lake, over which geese and herons fly—even a bald eagle every now and then. The shimmering lake is in view from the top of every part of the ramp. It's not uncommon for the especially talented rollerbladers to get so much air that it looks as though they might fly over the rails and plop right into the water.

Schmidty's began simply: with a single half-pipe. Over the years, it's expanded to include a double half-pipe with a spine, a half-bowl, a clamshell, and a volcano. Translation: it's a huge skateable surface with a lot of changing elevation, the kind of skate park where pros won't get bored and where beginners and intermediates will be pushed to their limits. Most recently, a narrow mini-ramp was added, and the Ramp & Camp patrons of spring 2021 were among the first to skate it. Adjacent to the ramps is a street section, with four different rails to grind. Schmidty's would be a top-rated skate park anywhere, which makes it even more impressive that it's on one man's private property, not maintained by the city or funded by tax dollars, as many skate parks of this caliber are.

I became acquainted with the ramps and my campsite before I met the eponymous Schmidty. When I asked around for Tim Schmidt, I was told, unhelpfully, "You'll know him when you see him."

But it didn't take long to spot the tall, lanky Tim. Two braids hung from either side of his helmet down to his waist, and he has so many laugh lines that he appeared to be smiling even when he wasn't. Yet from what I could see that weekend, he was always smiling. When I spotted Tim, he had a leaf blower backpack and was making sure the ramps were free of tree debris. Depending on the size of your wheels, the steepness of the ramp, and your speed and experience, even a leaf has the ability to take you down.

Each skate park has its nuances, its tricky spots, its weird little quirks that take a while to master and only a moment to wipe you out. I eyed the spine between the two half-pipes, which is unusual in that it's one big hunk of pipe instead of two smaller bars of coping back-to-back, when I spied my friend Siobhan, a rollerblader from Columbus.

"Watch out for that spine," she said, lifting her helmet to reveal a red gash across her forehead. "It's slicker than you think." I noticed the bruise on her eyelid, the bright purple of a grape juice stain.

Perhaps I wouldn't care so much or be as fearful about injuries if I'd started skating as a kid, like most of the rollerbladers at Schmidty's. It's not uncommon to hear someone who's visibly over thirty say, "I've been skating for twenty years" or, "I've been skating since I was eleven." But it hits different—literally—when you're a beginner as an adult. You've had years to contemplate your own mortality and cultivate a sense of fear.

That's a different philosophy than most of the rollerbladers have at Schmidty's. Having been to rollerblade events before, crashing them in my quads, I've seen a lot of aggressive rollerbladers who are truly fearless. With no helmet or padding, rollerbladers will drop in on ten-foot ramps, do spins and flips, bust their asses hard, and pop back up like it's nothing. During the competition portion of the weekend at Schmidty's, one competitor, Eddie Chun, fell and popped his shoulder out of socket. It appeared to all who witnessed it—an audible *oooof* rose up from the audience when it happened—that he would be out of commission. But a few minutes later, he popped his shoulder back into place and was able to get in a few more runs before his heat was over.

It's that kind of singular focus, eye-on-the-prize, do-it-anyway attitude that made Ramp & Camp possible. Tim grew up on the property that houses the skate park, which spans several acres and includes the mobile home park his parents own, where he works. He has lived there his whole life. Long before he built the skate ramps, he was just a kid running around the field, flipping his motorcycle off a hill.

"I started rollerblading on Purdue's campus at, like, thirteen years old," he said. "We didn't go to movies back then. A date would be like, let's go skate campus. When you're skating with girls, you're just trying to impress them by jumping over shit. That turned into grinding, then handrails . . ."

That's how skating is—it's a fairly quick progression from doing some cool tricks to skating becoming your driving force. At some point, it's not about the pursuit of new and bigger tricks but about being able to spend as much time on your wheels as possible. For people like Tim, who grew up in a rural area with no established skate parks for hours in any direction, and who got tired of being hassled by cops and property owners, often the only options were to give up skating or hit the road.

"Originally, I wanted a ramp at least this big or bigger," he said, pointing to one of the ramps at the park. "But I couldn't afford it, so I bought my camper van and just started traveling because it wasn't realistic to pay for something like this. It's ridiculous that my van was cheaper than this when it was a $30,000 van."

Tim and his friends took a 1973 Winnebago from West Lafayette to a skate competition in Atlanta, then drove to Louisiana and all the way to California, getting arrested in Tijuana along the way.

"We ended up skating through California and it was a forty-day trip. The gas mileage for that old Winnebago was insane. It was getting like eight miles a gallon and that was if we were going fifty-five. If we started going sixty, we'd get like four miles a gallon."

Tim has been all over the country rollerblading, but instead of putting down roots out West like many skaters have, he came back to his home, the literal plot of land his family has owned for his entire life. Instead of relying on skate spots elsewhere, he made one here, facing the challenges head-on with the gritty, DIY, devil-may-care ethos that's instinctive to skaters.

"If you don't have a place to blow off your stress," he said, "it gets weird. . . . It started off as fun, and it ends up just needing to do it to unwind. Mental health stuff. It's so easy to get mad at everything these days. But for people who exercise, there's this point where all your stress just melts away, and that's where I'm at in skating right now."

What was one skate park's loss was Tim's lucky day. The skate park he grew up skating in the 1990s and early 2000s, the one he had to drive hours to go to, went out of business.

"I got notified about the tear down, and I went in there and bought every single board and piece of metal I could. I salvaged something like two hundred sheets of ramp surface and four hundred feet of ramp coping. The retail cost of the materials alone would probably be $100,000," he said, still in disbelief all these years later. "That started the journey. . . . I tore down this beautiful, barely used skate park because it's just a fact of life: skate parks have a hard time staying in business."

Tim called a friend who knew how to build skate parks, and together, they built the spine in thirty-five days, finishing in October 2015, though they didn't get to enjoy their hard work for long before winter set in.

"Even an hour at a time, even at thirty degrees, it's amazing to skate," Tim said, smiling.

Tim wasted no time, and he started Ramp & Camp the next spring. Now there are two Ramp & Camps a year, one competition and one chill skate. Other groups organize events on the property in the meantime, and the local community is invited to skate. Carloads of skaters from nearby towns come nearly every weekend.

On Saturday morning, with a full day of skating ahead of me, I woke early—or rather, early for Ramp & Camp. Many of the bladers had partied into the morning's wee hours, the bass from the DJ's speakers rattling my tent flaps from a couple hundred yards away, so the majority of them had slept in late, giving me some time on the ramps with less traffic. No matter how many ramps I've dropped in on (or flung myself off of) I always get nervous the first time I drop in on a new ramp. I shake my body to rid myself of nerves like one might shake out a dream catcher to dispel nightmares.

I stepped over the edge and felt that moment of free-falling before my wheels hit the ramp surface and the rush of adrenaline kicked in like a drug. When I surfaced on the deck of the ramp, I saw Savannah, Schmidty's wolflike dog and the camp's mascot. Her ankles buckled from arthritis and age, so she teetered with each step, but her cream-colored fur was as full and soft as a much younger dog's. She was majestic, like a wise, mythical creature out of a fantasy novel. I climbed down, unable to resist a fluffy dog, and extended my hand to her. She gave it a tentative lick in the hopes I would offer her food, and it felt like I had been anointed. Like I and my misfit quad wheels belonged among the bladers.

Savannah is revered among the rollerbladers. When I asked Tim about her, his posture softened and he couldn't help grinning. For him, "man's best friend" isn't a trite old cliche—Tim loves Savannah with his whole being.

"My girlfriend gave me a dog for Christmas, so I started taking the dog out for fitness skating, and that turned into teaching her to jump over stuff. And that evolved into me just trying to take her everywhere with me," Tim said, remembering his travels to skate parks all over the country. "So back in 2005 or 2006, I went to Atlanta with a friend, who shot a photo where Savannah is jumping over the end of what we call a closeout rail. The rail is ninety degrees at the end, so I'm sliding one side of it and she's leaping over it. She's even got a smile on her face in the picture!"

The photo caught fire in the rollerblading community and was published in a blading magazine. Tim has a pristine copy of the issue with his and Savannah's picture bookmarked.

"My friend was saying, 'Dude, you're crazy,' but I'm like, no, my dog jumps over *anything*. She's even got a YouTube video from back in the day on my Dog Blader channel, where we're skating [Purdue's] campus and she's leaping over flowerpots."

I did the mental math and realized Savannah was at least sixteen years old. Looking at her ankles, which were wrapped in gauze and medical bandages, I wondered when the last time was that she had jumped over anything. I wondered if her body ached to jump like skaters' bodies ache for riding their wheels.

Savannah wove her way slowly around the ramps, stopping to oblige anyone who wanted to scratch her ears. A creature of infinite patience and affection.

Schmidty, in his graciousness, the god of this domain whom no rollerblader would deny, allowed an impromptu roller-skating competition. Roller skaters have shown up to Ramp & Camp in record numbers and there are so few roller-skating competitions that this felt like a historical moment.

One of the best aggressive quad skaters in the game right now, Bambi Bloodlust, was there, and although we all knew she would win, the rest of us didn't back down from the challenge. And there was money on the line. A guy hollered that he would give fifty dollars to whoever jumped from the handrail around the top of the ramp down to the incline, a space about three feet high and three feet out. Beyond that gap, the ramp itself is roughly five feet tall, so it would have been a three-foot free-fall onto a five-foot slide, totaling an eight-foot drop. Eight feet may not sound like a big deal, but only a cocky nonskater, an extremely skilled skater, or a completely reckless skater would tell you it's an easy trick.

Because Bambi was the most skilled among us, we all looked to her, trying not to pressure her but desperately wanting to see her do it. Not only to nail the trick, but to stick it to this guy who offered the fifty dollars, probably thinking none of us could actually do it. I wanted Bambi to prove him wrong. We all did.

The competition continued on with quad skaters doing jumps, spins, handstands, and cartwheels on the transition—gymnastic moves that the best rollerbladers incorporate into their own runs and, by extension, are forced to respect. As the minutes passed, the guy who had offered fifty dollars got impatient.

"I'll give one hundred dollars to whoever jumps off the handrail!" he yelled.

More time passed, and just when the crowd thought no one would take the triple-dog-darer's challenge, Bambi climbed the wooden handrail. She's an impossibly small woman with a mane of dark brown hair down to her waist like a pony. She balanced the handrail between the front and back wheels on each of her skates, raised herself to a tentative stand, balanced for a split second, and jumped. I let out an involuntary gasp. Her wheels hit the incline and when I blinked, she was back up the other side of the ramp, propelled by the speed from the jump. The crowd erupted into screaming cheers.

Later, I asked Bambi if the guy had given her the money. I'd assumed he wouldn't want to actually pay up and had just said he'd give whoever did the trick one hundred bucks because he didn't think anyone would do it.

"He did! He did!" she replied excitedly. "That's something that will culturally happen more at inline events. If somebody really wants to see a certain trick done, they'll start trying to entice their favorite skaters with a little payout. I think it's a funny motivator."

Even after my constant gripes at how quick people are to judge skaters, I'd done it myself.

Because male rollerbladers outnumber female and nonbinary rollerbladers, events tend to have a cultivated machismo. Rollerbladers, especially when there's a competition, will egg each other on to "get upside down!" and "the crowd's getting bored, so if you've been saving your big tricks now's the time!" and "do a backflip!" But I learned that those challenges are less about goading each other and more about issuing a friendly challenge. Whether or not the blader actually heeds the command doesn't matter. If they don't, cool. No one boos. No one is really disappointed. But if they do get upside down and do a backflip, that's when the performances get really fun.

And it is a *performance*. Among the skaters in each heat, you can tell who is skating for themselves and just so happens to be allowing others to watch, and who is a crowd favorite hamming it up for the spectators. I make these classifications without judgment; both types of skaters are rife with beautiful tricks and are entertaining to watch. "Beautiful" may seem like a strange descriptor for an activity called "aggressive" rollerblading and an "action" sport, but the bladers' forms are more elegant than one might imagine. So often, a trick can be done without paying much attention to form, but the trick can't be done well or without falling if it's not done elegantly. Landing a trick by the skin of your teeth and landing a trick well enough to make it look easy aren't the same thing. Elegance is a function of practice, patience, and time. Above all, elegance is a prime indicator of dedication.

I couldn't help but watch and wonder if I would have years of dedication ahead of me before my body broke down from age and use like Savannah's ankles. Then I heard the announcer say, "He's forty-seven and skates like he's seventeen," referring to one of the rollerbladers. I didn't know how long he'd been skating, but I hoped I have at least that many years ahead of me.

During the breaks between the competitors' heats, I looked closely at the construction of the skate park, knowing how much time, money, and sweat Tim and his friends had poured into it. Interestingly, I noticed it's not actually a permanent structure. Though it's hundreds of feet long, the ramp isn't dug into the ground but instead rests on cinder blocks.

"In our county, if you build a deck or structure bigger than a certain size and you use postholes, like if you dig holes in the ground and cement the poles, you have to have a permit," Tim explained. Though much has changed over the years, many municipalities still think of skaters as delinquent troublemakers and reject the idea of approving facilities for "riffraff." I could understand why Tim didn't want to go through the permitting process.

"We do have a handful of good parks popping up now, but for the most part, it's moderate support from the local communities in terms of wanting to build stuff for us. Like our town doesn't have an official public skate park. They've never been fond of skating in this town," Tim said, disappointed.

Thankfully, there are some other benefits to Ramp & Camp being built the way it is.

"It's easier to move a block when you fuck up. If you've never tried to block something before, it's really complicated to get your blocks in the right places and at the correct height. I've done a lot of blocking at the mobile home park, so it just made sense to do it in a similar way. And the higher the ramp is off the ground, the better you do with moisture," Tim said. "I've seen too many home-built ramps that rot apart because they're sitting on the ground or too close to the ground, and you can't get airflow under them. Keep it up in the air and keep the wind under it and it'll last a long time. If something breaks, you can even crawl up under it to fix it."

As the competition continued and bladers from their teens to forties took to the ramps, I thought about how the sport has changed over the decades. The older rollerbladers speak about the nineties like it was the heyday of blades. Having lived—and skated—through that decade, I asked Tim about rollerblading's evolution.

"It's not sustainable to jump off roofs and drop rails forever. To be honest, when we were doing that, we were doing it to prove a point that we weren't skateboarders and we could go bigger than skateboarders. That was the fucking essence of late nineties, early 2000s rollerblading," he said.

"Like, I don't know what we had to prove, but we were trying to prove *something*," he added, laughing. "Now, seeing our sport go into a technical phase with more controlled tricks, it definitely causes a divide in the community by all the has-beens who still think that skating should be die-hard big stunts. But it's also opening up a whole different element. Styles are evolving, and people are really doing more creative stuff. While it's not necessarily my style of skating, it's good for the industry in the long run."

It's then that I understood why Tim came back from his travels and built Ramp & Camp here. He built a facility that perfectly fits his style of skating, and because it's on his own land, his park isn't subject to the whims of other bladers. No matter where the sport goes or how it evolves, he will be able to skate exactly how he wants to skate, right in his own backyard.

"We're out here in redneck country. It's techno music, rock and roll, not your typical atmosphere. It's more about fun and being upbeat, not about trying to feel cool. Just vibe," said Tim, shrugging. "Experience nature and skating at the same time and be happy."

I watched Tim skate. He rolled with practiced grace, not unlike the geese that flapped over the lake behind him. Tim's braids bounced off his shoulders and back when he got air off the top of the ramp, and it looked like he was flying too. It would be wrong to say Schmidty's is in the middle of nowhere, because "nowhere" is still somewhere. And "middle of nowhere" sounds too much like the pejorative "flyover country." Schmidty's land has always been a "somewhere," but he's turned it into a destination. Or, if "flyover country" it must be, let us fly over ramps, over lakes, defy gravity on wheels, and soar.

St. Louis, Missouri

SK8 LIBORIUS

I spotted the spire through a gap in the trees over a block away and got chills. Sk8 Liborius, a skate park in the former St. Liborius cathedral, which was finished in 1889, cuts a sharp, Gothic image against the gray sky, heavy with impending rain.

Cathedrals aren't tiny structures, but Sk8 Liborius looms particularly large. Across the street, with my back up against the brick of the building opposite, I still couldn't fit the entire facade of the church in a single camera shot. Try as I might, the pictures don't do it justice anyway. I've seen plenty, however, because Sk8 Liborius is a bucket-list skate park. And ascending the stone steps through the tall double doors, you immediately understand why. Stripped of its pews, the floor opens to an expanse of ramps, including a tall vertical ramp made possible by the cathedral's height. The marble columns hold the buttressed ceiling.

I used to play a game with skaters and nonskaters alike where I'd show them a picture of the inside of Sk8 Liborius and ask them where they thought it was. Out of the ones who didn't know the place already, most said somewhere in Europe and some said New York City. When I announced it was in St. Louis, I knew their jaws would drop. They always did.

I want to believe the shock is from realizing Sk8 Liborius is closer than they thought. For skaters in the US, St. Louis is fairly centrally located, much more accessible than somewhere you can only take a plane or boat to reach. But I know better. People are surprised that something this cool is in the Midwest. After all, if people expected something like Sk8 Liborius to be here, wouldn't they have guessed that when I asked them where they thought it was?

Though I haven't been to mass in nearly a decade and only went as a child to please my grandmother, cathedrals always strike awe in me. The tall ceilings, the columns, the way the sound echoes on the tiles, the baroque paintings of the Stations of the Cross, and, of course, the stained-glass windows—all of it makes me feel small and the world feel more expansive.

That is to say, Sk8 Liborius felt holy when I entered it for the first time. Not in a specifically Catholic or even religious sense but in the way that skating can be a kind of religion. I've heard skaters describe it as their sanctuary and their refuge. A cathedral is a monument to human artistry and dedication. They're not easy to build; it takes a lot of time, years on end, and a lot of resources to bring a one to life, and then you have to work hard to maintain it. Skating is not altogether different. It's not easy to do, it takes years of dedicated practice to get good at it, and it requires an investment of time and resources. And anyone who's ever built a ramp and maintained it for years will tell you about the constant struggle and expense.

Perhaps there's someone who can look upon Gothic revival architecture and feel blasé about it, but that person isn't me. When I walked inside Sk8 Liborius, my eyes traveled upward through the vert ramp to the ribbed vaulting on the ceiling, the Corinthian columns, the clerestory with its stained-glass windows, and then back down to the altar, which held a speaker blasting rock music. Between the strumming of an electric guitar, itself another kind of shredding, birdsong echoed through the cavernous room. The cathedral's broken windows invited birds in, and Sk8 Liborius, like an airport or a Walmart Supercenter, is also a large birdhouse. Though their nests, situated past the dangling construction lights, were too high to spot, I could guess where their nests were, based on the splatters of dried bird poop on the ramps.

The poop doesn't take away from Sk8 Liborius's beauty, though—it only adds to it. Skaters have always had a gritty, DIY ethos. As a rule, skate parks are expensive to build and maintain, and that's especially true for one that's housed in a building that's over a century old and on the National Register of Historic Places. When St. Liborius was built in the late nineteenth century, the Dakotas, Montana, Washington, Idaho, Wyoming, Utah, Oklahoma, New Mexico, Arizona, Alaska, and Hawaii weren't states yet.

Slappy Sinclair, a skateboarder who's been shredding the streets and ramps of St. Louis for thirty years, put it another way: "They started building the church before Abraham Lincoln was born and didn't finish until after he was assassinated."

Sk8 Liborius looks like it's still under renovation because it is. To maintain a skate park that's not made of concrete is to constantly be renovating, fixing, patching. Tools lay off to the side, and wooden boards and bricks wait in the wings. More than anything, Sk8 Liborius is a labor of love. The near homonyms of "Liborius" and "laborious" did not fail to reach my ears.

This labor of love continues under the twenty-five-thousand-square-foot skate park. In the basement is the Liborius Urban Arts Studios, a makerspace and community arts center. It's through this nonprofit arm that Sk8 Liborius gives back to the community. As the organizers observed, "Skating is an activity that speaks across social, racial, and economic lines. You might come from a broken home, be poor and only own one pair of shoes, but you can be the coolest kid in the skate park because you put in the hard work and practice."

I met up with two local skaters there. Dee Drenning is a queer mom, veteran, pole class and burlesque instructor, printmaker, hula-hoop dancer, event organizer, mural painter, and all-around multidisciplinary artist about town. Elexus Adams is a nonbinary musician, makeup artist, and kawaii idol enthusiast, which involves a blend of cosplay, cheerleading, and karaoke. Both are talented ramp skaters and both have a practiced grace in their movements—Dee from her burlesque and pole classes and Elexus from their kawaii performances. Some skate forcefully with a "full send," do-or-die leap into obstacles, but Dee and Elexus are more like dancers elegantly navigating the rise and fall of each surface. Both grew up skating at roller rinks, and in the past two years, they've tried their skills on ramps. And both, through their connections in the community (including participating in rolling protests against the police as part of the Black Lives Matter movement) have gotten plugged into the city's skate scene at large.

"When we come together, it's the link up. It's all love," Dee said. "I don't really see much beef between people. Okay, maybe *a little* with the skateboarders."

"We just had to learn to assert ourselves," Elexus said.

When you're new to a hobby or sport, there's pressure to prove yourself, prove that you belong, prove that you deserve to take up space on these ramps, especially when the wheels you prefer are outnumbered by those of the far more popular skateboarding denizens.

As Black skaters, I imagine this is even more challenging if it's mostly white people on the ramps you want to skate. St. Louis is adjacent to Ferguson, Missouri, where Michael Brown was murdered in cold blood by Ferguson police in 2014. At intersections throughout St. Louis, there are blue and red flashing lights on the light posts and what look like megaphones perched atop the bars from which stoplights hang, a constant reminder that this is a city under surveillance. It's a reminder that the city's Black population is vilified, feared, and preyed upon by those who are supposed to serve and protect.

Skating history is Black history. Skating, particularly roller skating at rinks, is a glorious, thriving culture on its own, one that's deeply important to Black people in St. Louis and beyond. However, as I learned when I met Dee and Elexus, there are a number of Black quad skaters who skate both rinks and ramps. And since many talented jam skaters (those who dance on skates) don't use toe stops, Dee rides the ramps without the benefit of the brakes that so many roller skaters have. The challenge forces her to learn new ways of navigating and, of course, stopping. Without toe stops, her tricks and movements are more akin to inline skating.

St. Louis has two rinks that Dee and Elexus frequent: Skate King and Coachlite. For ramps, they gravitate toward Ramp Riders and the legendary Sk8 Liborius, the narthex of which we sat in to chug water and recoup from trying to start at the bottom of the vert ramp and see how high up we could get. While these spaces are integral to the local skate community, they are especially necessary due to the city government's hostility toward skaters.

While Dee and Elexus appreciate the rinks and indoor skate parks, all those parks are privately owned and charge admission to enter, which can be barriers to accessibility.

"It would be nice to have more skate parks in the city that are outdoors and that would be more accepting of the roller skaters," Dee said. "The skaters are hella accepting, but in the park rules, it'll say no roller skating on the sign. It'll also say no scooters, and I'm like, is the park only for skateboarders then?"

The signs don't stop them from trying, though. A public skate park, they reason, should be open to the public.

"Sometimes, when I go to Maplewood Skate Park, somebody's mom will want to say something about my roller skates and it'll be a whole thing," Dee said.

"It's for the children!" Elexus said, arms waving dramatically in mockery of the helicopter parents.

"There are some outdoor rinks around town that are nice, like the one at Loretta Hall Park. It's in the hood, and I love being there because I love that it's in that community," Dee said.

Many of the city-funded and city-maintained public skate facilities are not in St. Louis's Black neighborhoods. If you can't afford to skate at one of the indoor spots, and if there are few, if any, public skate spaces in your area, you're forced to skate in the street or on private property. Skater run-ins with cops have been widely documented, but for Black skaters, particularly in a place as rife with police brutality as St. Louis, running afoul of the police can be a death sentence. Accessible skate facilities can be a matter of survival.

"I know it was kind of a push for them to make Loretta Hall Park and the rink there. They really had to push. Meanwhile, they made the skate park in Maplewood, and that wasn't too much of a thing. Maplewood is an affluent neighborhood on the outskirts of the city. Loretta Hall is right downtown on the northside," Dee explained.

While both the Loretta Hall rink and Maplewood Skate Park were funded by tax dollars, an unambiguous fact is that it takes far more money to build a concrete skate park with a variety of ramps than it does to build a flat outdoor roller rink. The cost of the Maplewood Skate Park was paid for by $143,250 from the Municipal Park Grant Commission of St. Louis County, and that amount was $20,000 less than what was asked for. Concrete costs roughly $125 per flat square yard, so it's safe to say the cost of the rink at Loretta Hall Park pales in comparison. The city's enthusiasm to build one and not the other can hardly be explained without accounting for racism.

And though the Loretta Hall rink is a much-needed addition, it does little for people in the neighborhood who want to skate ramps. That's where Sk8 Liborius, the only skate park on the north side of St. Louis, comes in. It's just one mile, a mere three-minute drive, from Loretta Hall Park.

As Dee, Elexus, and I skated together, I felt that their inviting warmth reflected what I've seen of the skating community throughout the Midwest, though it stood in sharp contrast to the landscape of the city itself. In addition to the flashing police monitors on the light posts and megaphone announcers on the stoplights, St. Louis is almost bursting with gated communities throughout its neighborhoods. I passed so many, I lost count, and when my GPS led me astray, I found myself facing more than one tall iron fence, venturing a guess about who was inside the gates and who those inside wanted to keep out.

City planning is often a racist enterprise that, like most things in America, is routinely used to perpetuate white supremacy. Tactics include putting intentionally winding roads through wealthy neighborhoods so people who aren't from there and who appear not to know their way around can be easily targeted by police, and intentionally building interstates to bisect Black neighborhoods, displacing families and cutting off parts of the neighborhood from vital community, cultural, and economic centers. It's easy to forget, especially if you're white, that the roads and interstates we drive could very well have been built the way they are to terrorize Black communities. I tend to think of roads and even interstates as two-dimensional things that don't register on the visual plane in the same way a structure rising out of the ground does. It's much harder to forget that gated communities, replete with the actual and symbolic realities of gatekeeping, are also a product of racism.

The location and accessibility of public skate parks is both a function of city planning and racism. For whom is it acceptable to skate? Who is allowed to skate without barriers and threats of harassment from cops? When skating is a sanctuary for so many, it is city governments and city planners who decide which skaters get to partake in it. And when cops, security guards, and property owners run skaters off from whatever spots they manage to find, that sense of sanctuary can feel elusive, impossible.

On the Sk8 Liborius GoFundMe page, in which they're hoping to raise half a million dollars to restore the building and get more resources for the local kids they're serving through the nonprofit, the organizers had this to say: "Many teenagers feel that their life is going nowhere and that they lack any type of social or economic upward mobility. They tell us they need a third space. Not home or school, a third space. This is where Sk8 Liborius and the Liborius Urban Arts Studio steps in."

In contrast to so much of the city, Sk8 Liborius, which sits next to an urban garden, is a place not enclosed by gates. It's a formerly abandoned building in a neighborhood that I imagine many a white person has unfairly labeled "bad." It's a nonprofit that gives kids what they actually want—a cool place to hang out, a way to express themselves both physically and creatively, release aggression, develop a sense of community, and encounter people who care. Sk8 Liborius's doors stand wide open, welcoming all inside.

SKATE CHURCH

When you walk into Skate Church, you're not just walking into Skate Church. Housed in the same building, a former furniture warehouse now called the Center, are a number of nonprofits. There's Quad City Harm Reduction, which helps people who are addicted to drugs use them safely by giving people clean needles and Narcan. There's a donation-based coffee shop in the back. There's a food pantry and thrift store. There's a studio where they screen films and teach hip-hop classes. The sanctuary, which includes a low stage with a cross on top surrounded by folding chairs, is in the middle of it all. And in the very back is an indoor skate park, which sprawls across two floors through a maze of ramps and bowls. It's much larger than the pictures online would have you believe.

Pennie Kellenberger, who has been running Skate Church for twenty-one years, knows everyone in the Center by name. And they know her; she's the one they go to for help. It had been raining in Davenport the past few days before I visited, and one houseless man's quilt had gotten wet. He wasn't sure how he'd be able to dry it, since this was no job for a household dryer and it would likely need to be professionally dry cleaned, so they brainstormed solutions. Would the church dryer be able to dry out a quilt on site before it became irreparably mildewed? Probably not. Could they replace the quilt with other blankets? Pennie would check her supplies. She mentioned she'd just given away her last sleeping bag. She often gives supplies away the same day she gets them. Demand is high, supply is low, and the need is constant.

"Are your shoes wet?" she asked the man. He nodded.

"Take them off and dry them out," she said. The man looked a little unsure, as though he shouldn't be walking around barefoot in a church, but Pennie insisted that it would be okay, and he agreed. After all, Christian iconography often portrays Jesus barefoot. It'd be a hell of a thing for him to judge.

At the Center, "come as you are" is a philosophy that weaves throughout the organization. It's the same philosophy that led Pennie to start Skate Church over two decades ago.

"We kind of fell into it," she said. "We started doing skate ministry because I was working at the church across the street and I realized that the kids I was drawn to didn't fit the kids inside the church. They didn't feel as comfortable being inside the church, so we started doing things outside in the parking lot. They'd come with their skateboards, so we started building ramps."

What started as a few ramps in the parking lot became an indoor skate park at the church five years later. The process was organic. The kids were already skateboarding, and they brought their skateboards to the church parking lot of their own volition. Pennie, being a mom of two skateboarders, understands that what skaters want is a community and a place to practice.

"My son Justice was quite rebellious, but their dad and I made a commitment that we'd never take our sons' skateboards, *ever*. We'd take their phones or their game systems, but we'd let them go in the driveway and kickflip all day long. We never took their skateboards because we understood that they needed them," she said.

But what Pennie found is that by giving skaters the skate space they wanted, she also learned what they needed most.

"I don't skate, but I understand people who do. I understand people who are marginalized and in poverty," she said. "Here, that goes hand in hand. We wanted to create a place that's holistic. We talk about housing and education. We help with food and clothing and mental health—and we happen to have a really kickass skate park."

During the day, Pennie operates the Center—doing everything from writing grant requests to helping the people who sleep outside the door overnight get the assistance they need in the morning—but her heart is with the skaters. "What I really like is my night job, where I get to just open the skate park and watch kids skate," she said.

Pennie does more than watch, though. She listens. And sometimes, she's the only adult in a kid's life who does.

"I sit behind the snack bar and listen. I ask, 'How's your day? You get your work done? How's your mom?' One kid after another. They open up to me because I'm sitting back there at the snack bar. They sit down, get a Mountain Dew, and I ask how their day is and what trick they're working on. If they got the trick on film I want to see it," she said.

As we talked, I sensed that the Jesus Pennie knows and the Jesus I was taught about growing up are very different people. Pennie spoke of listening to the community, not handing down directives; of encouraging people, not vilifying them; of letting people be who they are instead of demanding they conform to some arbitrary idea of what a "good Christian" is. The skaters trust her because she's managed to make Jesus sound like someone who would have hung out with them.

"My purpose in loving people is faith-based. I fully respect other faiths, so you don't have to be any kind of faith to come into this place or into my life. It's just why I do what I do," she explained, adding that Skate Church is multifaith and nondenominational.

"I can't distinguish between everything we do here and the skate culture. I don't think every skater is going to be homeless, and I don't think that every skater is going to be entrenched in poverty, but here it works. We work with a lot of folks who are in the midst of housing insecurity, food insecurity, and other things going on in their lives. Some of them, the younger crowd, feel comfortable here because they know it's a skate park."

There are, of course, skaters who aren't in crisis who just come to skate. For those with more means, Pennie wants to make sure they understand that choosing to skate at Skate Church is an act of support for their peers who are in crisis.

"Skaters rally around a cause. That's the nature of a skater because they have this stick-it-to-the-man kind of attitude. So I talk to them about, 'Did you know there's so many people who came through the food pantry last month and you're helping? When you pay your four-dollar admission, it's helping to keep the food pantry going. You rock,'" she said. "I think skating changes the world because of the kind of people who like to skate."

As we talked, I kept expecting Pennie to ask me about my religion or what church I went to. I was thankful she didn't. I didn't want to tell her I'm an atheist, not when a desire to share God's love drives the lifesaving work she's doing. I didn't want to tell her that I was raised half-Catholic and half-evangelical Southern Baptist—expected in turns to follow prescribed rituals of kneeling and crossing myself *and* to speak in tongues from being moved by the spirit—and that my religious trauma runs deep. My aversion to faith comes from being made to confess, repent, raise my hands, testify, go down for an altar call, get told I was going to hell, swear to change my wicked ways, get baptized, get baptized again because one church didn't believe the other had done it right, then dedicate and rededicate my life to Christ. I didn't know how to tell her that an indoor skate park in Columbus, Ohio, is my church, just not in the way it is for the people of Skate Church.

But what I told her was this: If this Skate Church was plopped down in Columbus, I would go. What I told her is that I admired and respected her dedication to her community and that she did far more helping than preaching—the opposite of what I see most churches doing. I told her she walks the walk. My atheist ass would happily pay four dollars a session to skate a rad skate park where the funds go to support a food pantry, regardless of whether that food pantry was run out of a church.

If I believe skating can transcend boundaries and bring people together through a common love of conquering obstacles on wheels, how could I not also believe that skating could transcend the bounds of stuffy, traditional church to become a form of mutual aid? How could I not also believe that skating can, both directly and indirectly, save lives?

"One of the things I love about skaters is no matter where they go, they have a community. Drawing on your community is important, especially when you're in crisis. Jesus knew it. When you start to isolate is when things start to go bad for you. A lot of people think skaters are 'those radical kids,'" she said, using sarcastic air quotes. "But I really see it as a positive that they have a strong community."

Though Skate Church in Davenport isn't the first skate church (the first one was started in Portland in 1987), having been around since 2000, it's one of the earliest. Now skate churches dot the country, including several in the Midwest, like Truth Skate Church in South Haven, Michigan; Battleground Skate House in Battle Creek, Michigan; Skatechurch Grand Rapids in Grand Rapids, Michigan; and Skatechurch KC in Kansas City, Missouri.

Brandon Baker of Skate Church Movement, an organization that wants to unify and spread skate churches, is driven toward the work by how many times his skateboarding was incongruent with church settings.

"I think of all the times I've been kicked out of the church because I showed up to skate there—whether they like it or not, they build a lot of good skate spots outside churches—but they kicked us out because they think we're trying to destroy it. But in reality, we're just trying to do a practice," Brandon said. "I truly believe God gives us each passions that are ways for us to worship him, and for some of us, skateboarding is a way to worship."

Though I've never been formally kicked out of a church myself, I've been pushed out. I've suffered under the constricted teachings to the point that I've felt ready to burst. I wanted to expand my mind and experience to accommodate more of the world, and the older I got and the more I learned, the more church made me feel stifled and restricted. I had too many questions, and the church offered too few answers. There came a day when I couldn't abide another minute in a pew, another nosy question about my walk with God, another sermon where I was expected to be complicit in teachings I no longer believed in. Even so, it seems antithetical to everything a church teaches to kick a skater off the property when they could be invited inside instead or at least given a word of welcome.

"There's this weird divergence that doesn't allow us to understand each other, so it's caused a lot of separation between the church and the community. And with skateboarders, we've taken it seriously, and a lot of us don't want anything to do with church because if we're getting kicked out, there's no opportunity for respect or for a relationship to grow," Brandon said. "That's why I believe in the Skate Church Movement."

Churches don't seem to struggle to understand how sports in general are a pathway to the holy. Both the Catholic and Southern Baptist churches I attended growing up had annex buildings with basketball courts, so they seemed to understand on some level that there's an integration between sports and going to church and communing with your similarly religious peers. The Baptist church even had a room off the court with shelves of those brown-booted, orange-wheeled, rentable roller skates. Some of my first memories of skating are rolling around on that basketball court, trying to avoid kids' missed three-pointers. So there was even a level of acceptance in the nineties between roller skating and church. Yet that same welcome is so often not extended to skateboarders. It makes sense to me why skate churches, specifically, exist while bowling churches, football churches, and curling churches do not.

"One thing skaters have in common is you can't stop them. Persistence is a personality trait that threads through every skater," Pennie said.

Skaters skate in defiance of the police, of the government, and of private property, so it only makes sense that skaters would skate in defiance of the church too. Institutions, no matter how much power they believe they have, cannot stop skating. They can either get on board (pun intended) with skaters or prepare for nonstop opposition.

Skate Church is a testament to the fact that if you listen to the people you want to serve, they'll tell you what they need.

"When we started, there wasn't a skate park in Davenport," Pennie said, although one was built about ten years after Skate Church was established. "But my goal isn't to build skate parks, it's to build up people and communities. I didn't set out to build a really cool skate park, I set out to build really cool people."

I don't believe in much, but I do believe in skating. I believe in the wind on my face when I go down a ramp. I believe in sweat dripping down the small of my back and pooling under my breasts. I believe in knee pads and helmets, compression socks and freshly cleaned bearings. I believe in doing a trick you've been too scared to try for months and feeling powerful when you realize you have the skills and just needed to dispense the fear. I believe in falling and immediately doing the trick again so I don't give fear time to settle in my bones. I believe there's something about skating that makes it feel bigger than it is, like it's a reason to live and a metaphor for life, like it's a calling beyond the mortal self.

It's enough to make me almost—*almost*—believe in God.

LAURIDSEN SKATE PARK

I arrived in the state capital of Iowa a week after it had held the grand opening of the largest skate park in the country. At a whopping eighty-eight thousand square feet of freshly poured, butter-smooth concrete that stretches along the Des Moines River, it's simply magnificent. Though many past Dew Tours have been in California, it's no wonder that Dew Tour 2021 was right here in the middle of Iowa.

For the uninitiated, Dew Tour is an action-sports competition sponsored by Mountain Dew that happens twice a year. Going strong since 2005, the summer competition is for skateboarding, and the winter competition is for snowboarding. The competition is an aspirational one— if you make it to Dew Tour, you're one of the best—but the stakes were even higher at Dew Tour Des Moines. With skateboarding slated to make its Olympic debut, the competition was deemed a qualifying event, the only skateboard qualifier in North America. Skaters weren't just competing for the Dew Tour title; they were competing for the chance to represent their countries on the international stage as well.

The competition was divided into two parts: park and street. Park is where skaters compete for the best runs in the bowl, which has a riser like a mesa in the middle with rails to grind and half-sunk Mountain Dew cans to hurdle. The street competition, despite its name, was also at the skate park. Skaters competed for the best rail grinds, stair jumps, and board-flipping tricks.

Spectator tickets were limited due to the pandemic, but I managed to snag tickets for all four days, so I got to see everything, including legendary and up-and-coming skaters like Nyjah Huston, Sky Brown, Letícia Bufoni, Samarria Brevard, Jordyn Barratt, Misugu Okamoto, Lizzie Armanto, Manny Santiago, and Zion Wright. I saw some of my favorite skateboarders do their best tricks: five-forties in the bowl, eleven-stair jumps, dropping in twelve feet like it was nothing, airing over the hips in the bowl as sure-footed as if they were walking.

Two nights in, I pored through the bios of all the skaters on the Dew Tour website, and from what I could tell, not a single skater in the men's or women's street or park competitions was from the Midwest. One of the best skate parks in the country had been built in the region, after seventeen years of effort from the local community and SkateDSM, a local nonprofit, and no professional skateboarders from the region were there to compete for the hometown crowd.

The next day, I parked myself in the grass on a slope overlooking the park competition and felt alternatively dismayed at the lack of Midwest representation on the global stage and guilty that I had gotten free tickets to watch one of the best skateboarding events in the world and was complaining. The weather seemed to mimic my mood, alternating between blazing heat with humidity coming off the river, overcast hoodie weather, and torrential downpours. Des Moines was really driving home the old regional adage: "If you don't like the weather, wait five minutes."

During the light rains, Dew Tour workers came out with towels to dry off the rails, squeegees to rake rain off the large Mountain Dew decals affixed throughout the competition area's flat surfaces, and long air tunnels like giant vacuum hoses to evaporate the water from the largest skate areas. While they worked, the commentators who were unable to call out tricks—*Backside boneless! Pop shove-it onto the hubba! Fifty-fifty boardslide!*—worked to keep the audience entertained.

"We need more contests at the amateur level at local skate parks," one said.

"For sure," echoed the other. "It's one thing to skate by yourself at your local park and another thing to have millions of people watching in person and online."

It made me wonder if the lack of Midwest skateboarders at the competition stemmed from a lack of access or opportunity. After all, Lauridsen Skate Park had just opened in time for Dew Tour, and because it was a world-class park, surely more competitions would be held here in the future. At some of the past Dew Tours, temporary skate parks were built just for the competition and torn down afterward, but Lauridsen is permanent.

I was sitting toward the front of the viewing area and had gotten there early, so I hadn't paid much attention to the other spectators. When I turned around, more than anything, I saw kids. *Lots* of kids. Which means they're seeing skate competitions early in life. With a $7-million price tag, the park itself is proof that the local government supports skating too—enough to make Des Moines a skate destination.

Athletes need access and opportunity to make it to the Olympics, and that's exactly what parks like Lauridsen provide. The Midwest may not have any inaugural skateboard Olympians, but I bet the region will breed the skateboard Olympians of the future.

At one point, the announcers said, "Show California what's up!" and it felt like the dawn of a new era. Maybe the midwestern skaters of the future, especially those who aspire to the Olympics, won't feel like they have to relocate to train. Maybe Lauridsen will have a ripple effect.

On Sunday, the last day of the tour, I learned that it wasn't just the Olympic qualifiers who made this year's event unique: it was also the first year adaptive skating was included in the competition. "Adaptive skating" is an umbrella term for the various kinds of skating disabled people do, and it includes everything from WCMX—wheelchair motocross or chairskating—to skateboarding with crutches, prosthetics, white canes, and more. Though adaptive skateboarding and WCMX are typically separate competitions, they were combined at Dew Tour.

I'd never seen adaptive skateboarding or WCMX in real life, so I was thrilled. I was even more ecstatic when I realized the adaptive competition was where all the midwestern skaters were.

Tia Pearl's journey to Dew Tour was a long one. She came to the event from Galena, Illinois, which is in "the far northwest corner of the state, as close to Iowa and Wisconsin as you can get and still be in Illinois." Tia grew up in the skate scene, first rollerblading on adjustable K2s with a grind plate, then riding BMX like her dad did, and then trying skateboarding. There's a reason she says skateboarding is her true love.

"I met skateboarders at the skate park in my K2s, and I always got a reward if I brought home good grades on my report card. Beanie Babies set the bar for what rewards cost when I was a kid," said Tia, a child of the nineties like myself. "I thought if I got all these As, then instead of Beanie Babies, I could afford a Walmart board. I got a Mongoose board but wanted a real board from a skate shop."

"The night before Valentine's Day, my mom was like, 'We can go to that skate shop in Orland Park,'" Tia said, referencing a Chicago suburb about half an hour from where she grew up. "I got to pick out everything— the deck, the grip tape, the trucks—and build a full complete. We rolled out of there at like 8:30 p.m., and my mom let me skate till 10:00 p.m., which was late for an eleven-year-old."

At the time, she slept on a mattress on the floor and remembers putting the skateboard beside her bed and staring at it all night. In the morning, she rode her new board to school—on Valentine's Day.

Tia continued skateboarding through high school. Even as her friends dropped off and gave it up one by one when they got cars, she remained dedicated. She took her skateboard to college and started skating around campus. When she dropped out in the first semester, she didn't have the heart to tell her parents at first.

"I'd wake up every morning at the crack of dawn and leave at the same time as I did before. I'd get home and say, 'Yeah, school was good!' when my parents asked," Tia said, laughing at her younger self. "I played that for like three months until I was brave enough to tell them I dropped out in October and don't have any grades to show. They were like, 'Where'd you go all that time?' and I told them I was just skating around the college."

Nothing was going to stop Tia from skateboarding—not cheap Walmart boards, not friends ditching the sport, not college, and certainly not nerve damage.

In September 2011, Tia had surgery to repair a hernia. After she was supposed to be healed from the procedure, she noticed her leg going numb.

"They kept saying, 'It'll go away, just let it heal,' but it wasn't going away. I was like, 'I can't move my toes anymore . . . now I can't move my ankle," Tia said.

Eventually, her entire leg was constantly in pain, "like someone is rubbing sandpaper on an open wound." It was a dark time for Tia. She wasn't able to skate like she did before, and she and her wife had moved to a new town so their son could go to a better school, but the new apartment they found was on the second floor. With Tia's chronic pain, she had trouble leaving the apartment. She'd tried skateboarding, but her injured leg was her planting foot; she could push, but balancing on the board was impossible.

In spring 2014, Tia discovered WCMX and wanted to try it. But it's hard to chairskate in just any old wheelchair—WCMX chairs are designed to withstand drops on ramps and are built with tons of suspension in the way that regular wheelchairs aren't. They're expensive and often custom-made, which was out of reach for her at the time.

But Tia is nothing if not resourceful. By then, she and her family had moved to Galena, which has a sizable skate park. She managed to get ahold of two hospital chairs and made a Frankenstein-esque hybrid. By August 2015, she was ready.

"I told myself, 'I'm going to drop in on the quarter-pipe,' and I did it. I dropped in on the three-foot, then the four-foot. I was like, 'This is it! I got this!' So I turned into this maniac in a hospital chair at the skate park doing things people would never do because there's no suspension. It's the worst thing to be in," Tia said.

Through the help of a GoFundMe, she raised enough money to get a rigid wheelchair, which was a step up from a hospital chair and would allow her to grind rails, though it still lacked suspension. She took that wheelchair to skate parks throughout the region, including Olliewood in Dubuque, Iowa, and filmed her skate runs, posting them on Instagram and tagging wheelchair companies. She wanted them to see her, and it worked.

Tia was offered a $5,000 WCMX chair with a sizeable sponsorship discount, and she was able to work out the rest via a payment plan. The chair arrived on October 1, 2016, and the first thing she did was pop wheelies and spin donuts, laughing when she fell over. The center of gravity is a lot different than it is with a typical wheelchair.

"I trained for six months and placed fourth in the WCMX Worlds competition, which was really sick!" Tia said.

As her WCMX pro career took off—getting sponsorships, invitations to more competitions, free stuff, magazine interviews, and a floor pass to the X Games to coach WCMX, where she met Ryan Sheckler ("This is crazy, I used to watch *Life of Ryan* on MTV," she thought at the time)—she never stopped thinking about skateboarding.

In 2019, not long after the X Games, Tia saw a gif on Facebook of an adaptive skateboarder using crutches to skate and knew she had to try it.

"I pulled a pop shove-it right away," she said. "I felt like maybe I wasn't meant to walk everywhere but I was definitely meant to ride a skateboard." After a competition in February 2020, where she competed in both adaptive skateboarding and WCMX, she began phasing out of chairskating.

As an atypical skater, Tia sees skate parks differently than most people, and she saw that most of the skate parks she encountered in the Midwest weren't as accessible to chairskaters.

"It was like I hit a wall with it. If you ride WCMX, you need flow bowls that start shallow and slowly go down. But here it's like you can go down a ramp then up a ramp and that's it. You can't get enough speed to do things like what Aaron Wheelz [the inventor of WCMX] is doing where he's throwing one-eighties out of a bowl because we don't have ramps like that. Ours is just a bowl, not a flow bowl," Tia explained, feeling defeated that she couldn't progress at WCMX the way she wanted to. "I was doing the biggest ramps in Galena, but it was doing the biggest roll-in then just rolling away. There's nowhere to go." (Discovering she could skateboard on crutches made many more obstacles at skate parks accessible to her.)

Though the skate parks near Tia aren't the best suited for WCMX, there are definitely some positive aspects.

"Skateboarding in the Midwest, the country Midwest where I am, is so much different than skateboarding anywhere else. I got a message from another adaptive skater this morning who's in Florida, and he was at the park around ten-ish in the morning and said it was packed," Tia said. "Meanwhile, I was at the skate park from 9:00 to 10:30 a.m. and it was empty. I almost always have the skate park to myself."

Once Tia got her invitation to Dew Tour, she trained five days a week while managing her chronic pain and keeping up with her work around her farm. She'd get her chores done in the morning, go to the skate park, then come back and work in the barn. She felt confident going into Dew Tour, and in addition to her intense training, she had a little help from logistics.

"Selfishly, this is going to be my first competition where I have the upper hand because it's a street competition. I've never had the upper hand before because it's always a bowl and a crazy vert that I'm not going to do because I didn't get to train for that. This time, I actually have the upper hand in a women's competition because it's street. Even the men's Dew

Tour, they compete at both street and park, but they put all of us women in street," Tia explained. "I don't know why women didn't get to do both. Maybe they thought we weren't going to have as big of a turnout as the men. They did invite as many women as men, but only half of the women who were invited agreed."

For Tia, who remembers watching the inaugural Dew Tour on TV in 2005, competing was a bucket-list dream come true. And her hard work paid off: she took first place. The commentators called her "the Technician" because she's such a technical skater, knowing exactly where her feet need to be placed to bend the board to her will. She executes every trick with the grace of a devoted longtime skateboarder.

Meanwhile, in men's adaptive, Dan Mancina, a blind skateboarder from Detroit, competed alongside Joey Murillo, an adaptive skateboarder and amputee who was the only Des Moines local in the entire competition. Like Tia, Dan's journey to Dew Tour was challenging.

"I wish I had more time for Dew Tour. I broke my collarbone in February and had to have surgery, so I could only skate for a few weeks going into it," Dan said of the competition, which was in May. "I still don't think I'm 100 percent."

Watching Dan compete, I could tell he was disappointed in himself. Every skater has those days where even your most practiced tricks just don't go right, and unfortunately, his competition day was one.

"I'm bummed on my skating performance, but it's all good. Nerves got me. I still had a really good time, and it was awesome to be a part of. It's the good stuff like that that helps share our story," Dan said.

So often, skate parks aren't built with any kind of accessibility measures, so the park is either unskateable or dangerous for blind and low-vision folks. Dan's specialty trick is grinding rails, which he's masterful at in a supportive skate environment.

"There wasn't anything for me to skate in Lauridsen. The flat bar was partly covered up by the DJ booth, so it was like, I'm fucked right now," Dan said.

Dan didn't get to explore all of Lauridsen Skate Park between the competitions and the sections that were open to the public, which were crowded, but from what he was told, there wasn't much that was accessible. Dan skates with his white cane, so obstacles need to be large and long enough that he has time to find them with his cane and then have time to get on them for a decent trick. It's a simple solution in theory.

"Lengthening obstacles and making the objects bigger is one easy way to make accommodations, but the larger an obstacle is, the more money it costs to build," he explained.

Even small skate parks can cost tens of thousands of dollars, so cost—in addition to skate park builders just often not being aware of the needs of blind and low-vision skaters—can be a barrier to accessibility.

While talking to Tia and Dan, I can't help thinking about that gritty, DIY ethos that's endemic to both skaters and midwesterners. It comes down to doing the best with what you've got, which both of them have certainly done. What could be grittier and more DIY than skateboarding with a disability? When the world tells these skaters they can't do things, they prove they *can*—and better than most abled people.

But in talking to them, I can't help wondering how things might be different if skate parks were more accessible and competitions more supportive. Who's to say how things might have turned out if Tia had had flow bowls to chairskate and Dan had had a twenty-foot flat bar to grind?

The past is unchangeable, but the future holds much promise. Since Dew Tour 2021 was an Olympic-qualifying event, perhaps one day when WCMX and adaptive skateboarding are added to the Paralympics, a future Dew Tour might be a Paralympic-qualifying event.

"I always tell everyone that skateboarding was my first love and my forever love," Tia said. "If there's anything I held onto for my entire life, it's this. This is what I was put on this earth to do. I tell myself, keep riding your skateboard, Tia, and you'll go places."

Red Wing, Minnesota

RIEDELL SKATES

An hour southeast of the Twin Cities is Red Wing, Minnesota, a small town on the Mississippi River, spitting distance from the Wisconsin border. It's what I imagine many small towns wish they still were.

There are theaters and amphitheaters, museums dedicated to the military and pottery, and if you're inclined toward snowy action sports, ski jumping, which was invented in Red Wing. There are hiking trails, biking trails, and a casino for when you crave the darkness of a windowless, air-conditioned room with endless drinks and endless potential. There's a cute downtown area with small businesses and local restaurants, including one called Let Me Cheese U. There, in a moment of reckless abandon, I ordered the lobster mac for lunch, trying not to consider the freshness of lobster served so far from an ocean as I sat surrounded by men in flannel shirts and steel-toed boots despite the summer heat. It was the best lobster mac I've ever had.

More importantly, Red Wing has jobs—and lots of them. It's a manufacturing town, and not just for the shoes that share the town's name. In addition to Red Wing Shoes, there's 3M, which makes Post-it Notes, Scotch tape, and N95 respirators among other random office, medical, and orthodontic supplies; there's D. L. Ricci/Enerpac, which makes industrial tools whose use or purpose is beyond my understanding (hydraulic torque wrenches, anyone?); the Bic/Koozie Group, which makes company swag, like branded pens and water bottles; and there's S. B. Foot Tanning, which has been in operation since 1872. I assumed S. B. Foot Tanning got its name from being makers of shoe leather, but I was wrong. The founder's name was Silas Buck Foot. Sometimes truth is stranger than fiction.

It's likely due to the town's jobs that its population—around sixteen thousand—has stayed consistent for the past three decades, even as so many other towns like Red Wing have grown smaller.

The town is also home to Riedell Skates, which was founded by a Red Wing Shoes employee in 1945. Compared to other manufacturers in the area, Riedell is small, with only about 110 employees.

Paul Riedell and his wife, Sophie, were from Winona, Minnesota, about an hour downriver from Red Wing, and they bonded over a passion for ice skating. They skated as a pair in competitions and were local champions. Later, Paul was hired as a foreman at Red Wing Shoes, where he worked for nineteen years, eventually learning how to make shoes. Paul and Sophie weren't happy with the comfort level or performance of ice skates on the market.

In 1945, he put his designs to the test, and the couple opened Riedell Skates in their garage. Paul went to work at Red Wing Shoes in the morning and ran Riedell Skates after hours. There were hard times, times when Paul couldn't pay his employees but managed to inspire them to stay for a month or two with no checks until he could get caught up. In the beginning, they made custom skates for individuals, then word of mouth traveled, and Paul got his suitcase and drove throughout the region, drumming up more business. In the following years, roller skates were added to the assembly line—a natural fit for the company.

Today, Riedell-made ice and roller skates are shipped all over the world and are worn by everyone from hobbyists to Olympic ice skaters and roller derby pros. The company recently celebrated its seventy-sixth anniversary and is still family-owned and operated. Paul and Sophie

Riedell's four grandsons, Scott, Bob, Paul, and Dan Riegelman, run the company. I caught up with Scott, vice president of the roller division, at the company headquarters, where Paul's innovations are still the backbone of Riedell's designs.

"He didn't think ice skates had a proper fit, so after working with a local foot doctor to learn about the bones of the feet, he developed what's called a 'shoe last' or a 'skate last,'" Scott explained. A last is a wooden or plastic replica of a foot that informs how the boot is made. His grandfather's lasts are still the ones the company uses. They were integral to Riedell's success, then as now.

I couldn't help wondering if there was a rivalry between Red Wing Shoes and Riedell Skates now. I mean, Paul worked at Red Wing for nineteen years, learned all the secrets, then left to start his own company.

"No, not at all," Scott chuckled. "It was a good working relationship, and they were very kind to him." The two companies continue to have a good rapport. Riedell gets much of their leather from S. B. Foot Tanning, which Red Wing now owns, and there have been times when Riedell's business suddenly ticked upward and the shoe employees came in to help. Thanks to the pandemic, 2020 kicked off the single biggest and most rapid demand for roller skates in the company's history.

"It's wonderful to see it happening," Scott said. "When the pandemic started and the regulations had everything closed, we were shut down for seven weeks. We didn't know how we were going to keep the employees, how long they were going to be off, and there weren't any orders coming in. Most of the ice rinks in the country are owned by city parks and rec, and that was 100 percent closed. And around the country, each state made their own ordinances on roller rinks, and the majority of them were shut down," Scott added. "Who would know during the pandemic with health clubs shut down, everyone wants to be outside roller skating!"

Though this recent spike in roller skating interest is the biggest in the company's history, the demand isn't without precedent.

"I've been here forty-five years, and [in] tough times, roller skating is always elevated," Scott said. "Because it's an inexpensive sport for families, it's affordable to go to rinks if they're open, or there's parks everywhere to roller skate in. Skating is freedom."

And who doesn't want a sense of freedom, especially when the state of the world is uncertain?

Though it was a good problem to have, the pandemic demand for roller skates overwhelmed the company, and some orders were out as long as twenty-four weeks. Riedell opened another skate manufacturing facility in Arkansas and hired dozens of new employees to get on top of the backlog.

The majority of Riedell skates are made in America (with a handful made overseas), though some of the parts are made in facilities around the world. Getting those pieces while the pandemic raged on was a challenge.

"The factories got so busy that there were power outages, and the government is shutting the factories down because they don't have vaccinations like we do. COVID is hitting pretty hard in China, Thailand, and Cambodia," Scott explained.

Riedell's US suppliers are also going through some of the same difficulties as the Riedell factory.

"You can't roller skate if you can't get wheels. We have two US manufacturers that are out six months delivering," he said. "It's hard to run a business."

Scott also mentioned that part of what made running a business complicated at the time I visited is that he believes a lot of people don't want to work, that as a result of the pandemic, people are happy to stay home and collect unemployment. I've seen the viral social media posts about bosses taping demeaning signs to the door about how they had to close for the day because "no one wants to work," yet it's almost always revealed that the bosses are terrible and the pay is minuscule. Though Riedell desperately needs more people to keep up with the demand for skates, Scott doesn't disdain his employees like the subjects of these viral posts, however. He greeted everyone we passed on the factory floor by name, and they seemed genuinely happy to chat for a moment about what they were working on, whether it was cutting the leather pieces for the skate boots, hammering in the eyelets, cementing the soles, attaching the wheels, or wrapping a pallet for shipping. Over the eighty-thousand-square-foot facility, Scott routinely pointed out employees who had been with the company for twenty-five years or more. When Scott told me he cared deeply about his employees, I believed him.

I didn't mention that I myself was laid off during the pandemic and that being able to get unemployment for several months was part of how this book came to be. I had the time, space, and energy to research the concept of Midwest skate history and put together a compelling enough book proposal that it got picked up by a publisher. I didn't tell him that if it weren't for unemployment money, I wouldn't be interviewing him.

There's a certain glamorization of manufacturing and factory work in our collective imagination in the US because, perhaps with the exception of the arts, manufacturing is a clear path to creation. The output of one's labor is tangible. What is created by one's hands leaves Red Wing and—through plane and train and car—finds its way to homes across America. The work itself may be grueling, prone to repetitive stress injuries, but the skill must be respected, and that creative aspect is rewarding—for some a little while and for others a lifetime. I didn't have the heart to tell Scott that I was one of the unemployed masses that would not be tempted by this or any other job, not right then and likely not ever again, even as I longed for a new pair of skates that I knew will take the better part of a year to make. Maybe it's foolhardy of me to think I can be a full-time writer, but it's the form of creation I'm best at, and I can't help wondering how many other of the unemployed masses are like me, using their unemployment checks to stay alive long enough to figure out how to make their dreams feasible.

It is easy in our capitalist country to tie the ability to provide for oneself and one's family to self-worth. We ask children what they want to be when they grow up and expect them to respond with an answer relating to labor. What we're really asking is, which method of selling your time, energy, and body seems most appealing to you right now? I don't know anyone who *wants* to work, per se—I only know people who desire to create. Perhaps that creation element is part of why Riedell workers stay with the company for decades.

"Everybody works together. We have weekly meetings up front and discuss everything business-wise with all of our people. We're family-owned, and that's how we want to run it, so everyone is involved. We have a suggestion box in the lunchroom, and we read them once a week and talk about them. We're not trying to be corporate America," Scott said.

Given the pandemic, the workers on the manufacturing floor were spaced out. Scott gave me what he called the "twenty-five-cent tour," an overview of the facility without getting too close to the employees, all of whom were wearing masks.

We began in the cutting department, where dyed leather hides and vegan manmade materials are checked for imperfections, then cut into shapes to form the sides of the boot and the tongue.

"Leather is one of the most expensive things in the boot," Scott explained. "We look for imperfections like where the cow rubbed against a barbed wire fence, brands, and veins."

Rather than scissors, the cutters use overhead cutting machines. A sheet of leather is placed on a table, then the cutters place metal frames in the shape of the boot parts on top. Then they pull down the overhead machine to apply enough pressure to the metal frame to make the needed cutout. The process is like an industrial version of using a cookie cutter.

I observed Helen as she pulled the overhead cutter down and it made a noise like a big hole punch. Scott told me she's worked there for forty years.

After cutting, the pieces go to the fitting department, which is all stitching—everything from putting the lace hooks on the top of the boot to sewing the liner and label. Rows of antique Singers lined the room.

"Some of these old Singers have been on our line for probably seventy-five years, and we've got a hundred of them," Scott said.

Riedell has their own line of skates, and they also manufacture skates for brands like Moxi and Antik. Scott can tell just by looking at the pieces which kind of skate someone is working on. He points out who's working on what as we pass. Though he told me some parts of the shoemaking involve computerized stitching—done by machines that cost upwards of $40,000—I'm still in awe of just how much hands-on stitching goes into each boot.

Once the parts are sewn together, they go to the lasting department, where the pieces are fitted over an appropriately sized shoe last—the ones Paul Riedell created all those years ago—to do some additional stitching and really cement the boot together. In the bottoming department, the soles of the boot are nailed in and, using a machine that costs roughly $150,000, workers heat the toe box to mold extra support onto the boot.

Next is the finishing department, where the mechanical components, like the plate, kingpins, axles, wheels, and toe stops are added before a final inspection. I watched in awe as multiple pairs of my dream skates, the ones I've been saving up for, have their hardware screwed into place by many pairs of capable hands.

Lastly, Scott took me to the shipping department, the final stop before the skates are sent to the shops who sell them. There's a long line of cardboard boxes, dozens upon dozens, all of which were destined to leave the warehouse that day.

"What's in these, Ben?" Scott asked a man with a clipboard.

"Materials for the Arkansas facility," he replied, and Scott nodded approvingly.

"That's good," Scott said to me. "We've got eighty thousand square feet here and we're running out of space."

Another worker drove by on a machine that wraps a pallet piled high with boxes of skates in plastic so they don't tumble during transport.

"Hi, Jeanie," Scott said as he waved to her. "Where's this one going?"

"Kansas City!"

"Alright, don't get dizzy!" he called back. She laughed.

It's hard to say exactly how long it takes for a single skate to be made. Each pair requires over one hundred individual steps to create, and the custom models and pro models require over two hundred. For efficiency's sake, Riedell makes the skates in assembly-line fashion, a handful of sizes at a time, and if there are no hurdles—like a delayed shipment from a supplier, a vital machine breaking, or a COVID-induced shutdown—a pair of off-the-line, noncustom skates can be made in seven to ten days. To those who are eagerly awaiting their orders to come in, this may not sound like a long time, but with demand so high and a backlog of orders waiting to be fulfilled, and with the supply chain issues stemming from the pandemic, things can take a while.

Though the demand was spurred by people wanting to skate outside during the pandemic, it's hard to know how many of these new skaters only wanted to skate outside versus how many would be using their new skates at skate parks. Park skating hasn't historically been part of the repertoire of sports Riedell has emphasized; the company has mostly focused on rink skating and roller derby. I asked Scott what he thinks of the new interest in skate parks.

"It's the fastest growing thing right now. We can't keep those in stock," he said, gesturing to packages of Community In Bowls slide blocks, which can be affixed to roller skates to allow the skater to grind ledges, rails, and coping. "There's a trade show called RollerCon that's a gathering of roller derby skaters. It's primarily women who gather once a year in Las Vegas, and we always go to that. There are a lot of derby-driven classes, but they also do classes on fun skating and ramps. At the last gathering, there was a ramp, and you had to wait to get on it, so we saw the trend coming."

Forecasting roller skating at skate parks also pushed Riedell to grow in other ways. They hired Bambi Bloodlust (real name, Katie Baird, who you may remember from Schmidty's Ramp & Camp) as their creative director.

"It's my dream job," Bambi said. "I started out doing freelance work for the Moxi brand, like an illustration for a skate lining, a T-shirt graphic, or stickers. I was working for an ad agency in Chicago and doing Moxi projects on the side. I enjoyed my agency job, but it was time-consuming and hard to get time off for skating events, so it was hard to balance."

Michelle Steilen, who created the Moxi brand by asking Riedell to make lifestyle skates in bright, fun colors, opened the door for Bambi to get a full-time job at Riedell.

"Before me, they didn't really have anybody in-house overseeing all the creative, and they were outsourcing every project across their brands, so as you can imagine, that would get disjointed," Bambi explained. "So I came in and started doing a lot of the graphic design and marketing."

Riedell has experienced so much growth over the past couple of years, though history has shown that while roller skating never goes away, it does have cycles.

"It's not going anywhere in the near future," Scott said. "Things will slow down because what happens in any craze is everyone takes a look at a hot market and floods the market. So we know it will slow down, but it'll slow down, and the major brands will hang in there. We know we won't be this busy for another two years in a row, but we'll see another year out of it for sure, which is terrific."

As nerdy as it might sound, being in the Riedell factory felt magical. Seeing the wide sheets of leather before they were cut, hearing the repetitive sounds of compressed air machines, beeping forklifts being thrown into reverse, and the hum and growl of manufacturing, was oddly soothing. I've owned multiple pairs of Riedells throughout my life, from my derby skates that I used for years at the rink near my hometown in Alabama to my current skate park setup. Seeing the place where they're made and the hands that created them made me appreciate my skates even more.

The factory made me nostalgic for something I'd never really seen before my visit to Red Wing. The last time I saw a factory, it was a steel plant in my hometown, and I watched hot steel beams roll off a conveyor belt into neat piles. I saw a vat of slag that looked like molten lava, a pool of neon orange. Of course, there were people operating the machines to make the steel, but the nature of the product didn't lend itself to handmade craftsmanship. So much safety gear was necessary that you couldn't see most of the workers' faces through welding masks and hard hats. They could have been robots and I would've been none the wiser. And though steel beams are vital parts of architecture and infrastructure, they're never something I look at with real gratitude and curiosity, nothing like the way I look at my skates, a thing I can hold in my hands and that attach to my body like an extension of my limbs. Though it could be argued that steel beams do more good for the world than skates, I will never look at steel with affection. I will never look at steel and think of freedom. I will never look at a steel beam and consider the artistry that went into it, the many hands that made it before it became mine.

"We're bringing some things back from overseas that we think we can do better," Scott said. "We take pride in what we do."

THE SHRED SHED

If you don't already know where the Shred Shed is, you'll never find it. Your GPS will lead you in circles, instructing, "make a U-turn" until you're dizzy. But forty minutes outside Madison, after the rolling hills turn to gentle waves of green, past a statue of a Pepto-Bismol-pink elephant wearing sunglasses, in a town whose sign says it has a population of 833, is a secret DIY skate spot.

As I entered the maze of warehouses (I've sworn not to share the exact location), I felt like I was heading into the skate version of Fight Club. *The first rule of Shred Shed is you don't talk about Shred Shed.* . . . But that's not exactly it. Though Madison has several excellent outdoor skate parks, the city doesn't have any indoor parks, so skaters are out of luck in the winter unless they're willing to make the two-plus-hour trek to Milwaukee to go to Four Seasons or Cream City Skate Park. The only indoor places to skate around Madison are secret DIY spots, hidden in the most unlikely places.

My entrance to the Shred Shed came courtesy of Melissa Frazier, whose skate name is Tuna Fey and who serves as one of the Shed's organizers. She maintains the ramps, collects dues from keyholders, and works with the original founder, Sepi Shokri (aka Neon), to ensure the rent for the space gets paid. She greeted me warmly in the parking lot;

there was no signage, and it was impossible to tell which of the many warehouses in the area was the place I was looking for.

We entered one and went down a long hallway to a room with a maze of pallets piled high with white bags. There was an earthy, natural scent in the air.

"When you smell the mulch, you're getting close," Melissa chuckled.

The Shred Shed's neighbor in the space is a landscaping company, where they store bags of lawn accouterments. Weave around a little more and in a back corner against a brick wall, there it is: two mini-ramps, a ledge with PVC coping, a mini-spine, and a quarter ramp. Melissa removed the plastic sheet that covered one ramp and a storage tub used to catch rain from the leaking roof. Skaters who have visited the space write their names, both real and skate nicknames, and words of encouragement on the brick wall dividing the Shred Shed from the warehouse's other rentable spaces.

The Shred Shed's secrecy isn't meant to be unwelcoming—Melissa and the other keyholders want people to skate, and having new skaters in the space brings them joy. But they also know that the downfall of many a DIY spot has been members who don't pay dues and nonmembers who use the space but don't donate. Keyholders get frustrated that it's too crowded, and soon, the organizers aren't able to make rent. Rather than Fight Club, the Shred Shed is more akin to the Virginia Woolf quote, "A woman must have money and a room of her own if she is to write fiction." Money and a room of one's own is exactly what it takes to run a longstanding, sustainable DIY skate spot.

The DIY Cassady Bowl in Columbus closed because not enough of the skaters who used the space paid to skate there—the door code was given out indiscriminately. Having recently come from St. Louis, I'd heard half a dozen people lament the DIY spot under the old Kingshighway Bridge that got torn down when the bridge was razed and rebuilt. I think of the countless other DIY spots that have been torn down by local governments, that have fallen into disrepair from lack of funds, or that have become unusable due to cops patrolling the area and property owners cracking down. Though it's always possible that the landlord of a rented space could raise the rent to the point of forcing a skate park out, one thing is clear: either-or will not do. Skaters need money *and* a room of their own to build their own spot. Skating a skate park, especially if it's a secret DIY spot, requires the freedom that money and space can afford—and that's what the Shred Shed has.

Melissa's path to ramp skating—and ramp building—was circuitous.

"I wanted to be Tara Lipinski when I was really young," she laughed. "I learned how to roller skate on a field trip as a kid and thought if I can roller skate, maybe I can figure skate. That didn't work out. I have hips."

In 2012, she attended her first roller derby bout to support her partner's coworker who was on the team. Though she didn't know much about the sport—she had to read the rules on Wikipedia as the bout progressed—she was intrigued.

"I realized I wanted to do this. This is really badass. I'm getting to watch all these people do something so athletic and exciting, and they seem to have this camaraderie that is so beautiful. They're fierce and strong and I wanted that," Melissa said. "But I thought I wasn't cool enough to do this sort of thing, so I put it out of my head for a while."

Eventually, the call to don skates was too strong to ignore, though. She bought skates and tried out for the local derby team, which was then called the Mad Rollin' Dolls. (It's now called Madison Roller Derby to be more gender inclusive.) After being accepted into the draft pool bootcamp, Melissa worked all summer to improve her skills in the hopes of being drafted for the team. She did this all while also planning her wedding. And by the end of the summer, her hard work paid off.

"The draft night was actually on my wedding night. I let the team captains know once I found out I was getting drafted and said they can come to our wedding if they wanted. No pressure, obviously, it was going to be an exciting night for everybody. But they did end up coming and it was so, so fun," Melissa said, a happy tear sparkling at the corner of her eye.

Over the next few years, Melissa played in dozens of derby games, taught and encouraged younger skaters, got injured and retired, came out of retirement once she was healed, traveled to bouts both around Wisconsin and outside the state, and eventually retired again to make way for newer skaters who were enthusiastic about leading the team forward.

But after retirement, she felt there was something missing.

"When I stopped playing, I felt like I lost a piece of myself and my identity," she said.

In 2016, there was a roller derby convention in Madison that included a skate park day, and Melissa went.

"I tried out Madison's Central [Park] skate park for the first time, and it was exciting. It was fun, and I think I gave myself a concussion from banana peeling," Melissa said. "I stayed off skate parks for a while. Then in 2018, some folks came back to do a skate park tutorial."

That tutorial was led by Sepi, a former derby player herself, and that session planted the seed for what would become the Shred Shed. Madison is fortunate in that it has several outdoor skate parks, but not having a public indoor skate park in a place that gets as cold as Wisconsin does often means skaters are forced to take a break during the coldest months.

"We'd talked about it over the summer, like what do we want to do when winter comes? Wouldn't it be great if we could have a space for when everything is closed or it's freezing out or even when it's raining in the summer? Then Neon was like, 'Why don't we make our own?'"

To be a skater is to be a dreamer. To do a sport that is wholly impractical and try to fling yourself skyward through wheeled propulsion is nothing if not the product of dreaming about what could be under the right conditions and with the right resources. Yet Melissa didn't entirely believe something like the Shred Shed would really happen.

"It was like, okay, sure, that sounds good. . . . I'm excited but I'm trying to be realistic. It's really a big endeavor," she said, eyes wide. "Looking back, I can't even believe I questioned it."

Finding a space to rent was only the first step. A small group of early keyholders, many of whom had never built ramps before or even used power tools, put their heads together to build one of the two mini-ramps in the space—affectionately named Ramp Randall after Camp Randall, the football stadium at the University of Wisconsin. To get money for the materials, the keyholders had to fundraise.

"We sold patches," Melissa said. "It was really exciting that people wanted to support what we were doing. . . . This is what it feels like to have the community rallying for you, knowing that this isn't something that happens all the time. Businesses go belly-up, nonprofits go belly-up, there's lots of recreational groups that don't pan out. So knowing that we had support behind us made it feel like it was possible."

The Shred Shed opened just in time for a launch party on New Year's Eve in 2018, so the keyholders celebrated by ringing in the new year on the ramps, something that, unless you own an indoor ramp, is nearly impossible to do in Madison.

Having somewhere to skate indoors during the winter isn't just "nice to have." For people who need to skate, people whose bodies crave the feeling of wheels under them, it's a necessity; without it, you'll lose a piece of yourself. That was especially true during the pandemic.

Like Melissa, Natsuko Suzuki came to park skating by way of roller derby, but when derby was canceled due to the coronavirus, they started going to skate parks. They moved to Wisconsin four years ago from a small town in upstate New York where there weren't any skate parks.

"I'm Japanese and lived in a pretty white town. It just never seemed like something a young Asian girl would do," they said. "Like you see Tony Hawk and think, 'Yeah, this is cool,' but that's not my world. But now, seeing the Olympics, there are all these Japanese skaters that won in street skating and park skating, and it makes me think differently."

Though they were initially afraid of hitting people, what drew Natsuko to roller derby was that all the queer people in Madison seemed to be there.

"It was one of the first places I saw big, strong queer people and it was like, 'Wow, I want to be that.' That gathering of people was a powerful thing for me to see," they said.

There's so much crossover between the roller derby and aggressive quad skating communities that doing both seems like a natural fit.

"It was definitely a transition to get used to the different ways of moving your weight around without falling over and to learn how I could try new things and what was comfortable for me. How to face fear and be able to push through it in a way that I'm not really used to doing as an adult," Natsuko said. "I feel like it's a battle between trusting your body and your muscle memory with the knowledge that this is objectively kind of a dumb thing to do. I had to be able to make my brain trust my body. Being able to confront that fear in skating also makes me a braver person in normal life. I know how to confront things better now."

The crossover appeal of derby skaters going to skate parks also makes the park skating scene more diverse. All the things that drew Natsuko to roller derby get replicated on the ramps.

"I went to Waunakee Skate Park with Tuna and another friend, and there were three other roller skaters who were not cis men who rolled up. It was like, 'Wow, this is the first time I've been to a skate park where it wasn't *all* these guys and us," they said. "It's great to see other people enjoy skating and feel empowered to be in the skate park, which can be intimidating if you're not super good/a guy."

Both cited a regular meetup of femme and queer skaters on a variety of wheels as being an inspiration that helped them get more comfortable at the local skate parks. Still, there's a long way to go.

"Madison is pretty white. It's easy to tell people who I am if I'm trying to meet up with them because I can say, 'I'm the only Asian quad skater,'" Natsuko said.

In addition to beating the winter blues, part of the impetus behind creating the Shred Shed was that Madison needed an indoor space that could be a safe space for people with marginalized identities *and* that was open to a variety of wheels. There are other indoor DIY spots in Madison, but they may not be safe spaces for all people, or if they are safe spaces, they may only allow one kind of wheel, or they may be so secret that only a handful of people are allowed to skate there. There are a hundred ways to make a skate spot exclusive, and given the difficulty of maintaining DIY spots, there are compelling reasons for exclusivity. But there's an art to making a DIY skate park that's a safe space, open to all wheels, not so secret as to be inaccessible, *and* financially self-sustaining.

"We have bladers, skateboarders, and quad skaters," Melissa said. "It's neat to see how it's opened up the space and opened up the groups across the different communities of skating. Because I wouldn't have felt comfortable going to skate parks and just skating with skateboarders as the only quad skater. There's not another space like it in Madison that I'm aware of."

That's why Natsuko spent winter at the Shred Shed. Though both Melissa and Natsuko were derby skaters first, they came to love ramp skating in its own right. Despite the fact that the desire to skate ramps is present year-round, park skating in the Midwest so often follows the cycle of nature's seasons. Having a DIY spot, funded by sufficient money and housed by a sufficient space, is to defy nature, to keep winter from imposing its freezing will on your wheels.

"My friend is a keyholder, so we went a bunch, and that was the main place we skated when it was snowing. There's another DIY private spot in town, but the only one I have access to is the Shred Shed," they said.

The Shred Shed is a safe haven, a harbor from the winter storm and—at least metaphorically—a soft place to land.

"It made me think of myself as an athlete. My relationship with my body is better. I want to take care of it because I want to do a thing—not because I want to conform to some arbitrary standard of beauty. I do cross-training and do things that make my body feel good and eat better," Natsuko said. "With park skating, I'm better at listening to my body, like if I need more water or if I just need to stop. If you're tired, your feet aren't in the right place where you need them to be—then you'll hurt yourself. Me and my body are more in tune because of that."

"I've spent the past four years skating skate parks, and being able to do that is what helped me let go of derby. And I don't know that my transition would have been as smooth if I hadn't had this to come to, because I didn't realize just how much I loved skating until I wasn't doing it anymore," Melissa said.

The Shred Shed would be an enviable DIY spot anywhere because you don't get skate spaces like this without serious dedication and community support.

"The way I see it, the more attention that gets drawn to what we do here, not just in the Shred Shed but in the Midwest in general and our skate community here, is good," Melissa said. "There needs to be an awareness that people out here do want to skate, that we love this and have an appreciation for it and we want to share it with people."

LOGAN BOULEVARD SKATE PARK

I once heard a skater say that Chicago is the biggest city in the world not to have a decent skate park. (I'll avoid naming them to protect the guilty against the Windy City's wheeled denizens.) "Decent" is a matter of opinion, and I found it hard to believe that in all of Chicago's vast, sprawling, mass of a city, there wouldn't be a good skate park.

So I visited what some would argue is the worst skate park in the city: Logan Boulevard.

The Google reviews say it all.

> This is a last resort sort of place. It's covered in pigeon droppings which will get on your griptape. The layout is awkward and poorly constructed in addition to the wood rot and rust. I honestly can't recommend it.

> The ramps are degrading. The manual pad is cracked on one side. The quarter pipes are coming apart. Isn't there someone to maintain this place?

I feel like I could get injured at any time from a stray crack or broken ramp face.

Probably the worst in the city.

It sucks.

Trash.

Greg Roberts, who founded the skate collective Pardon My Thrashing and co-runs it with his wife, Maria Gutierrez, echoed these sentiments. "I won't go there," he said.

I reasoned that if I were one to heed warnings, I wouldn't strap wheels to my feet and jump off shit. And if I visited Chicago's worst skate park and found it "decent"—according to my own arbitrary standards—then that could only mean the rest of the skate parks in the city were even better. Very scientific research.

Located under an overpass, Logan Boulevard Skate Park isn't the easiest place to get to. The street below is a busy thoroughfare, and there are signs on nearby streets and buildings warning you not to park there if you don't live there. I ended up parking at a movie theater garage and walking a third of a mile to reach the park, which hardly warrants mentioning if you weren't carrying seven pounds of skates, half a gallon of water, and a duffel bag full of pads like I was.

Rounding the corner of the thoroughfare, the overpass came into view. The park under it was shady, perfect for those blazing hot Chicago summer days where the humidity rolls off Lake Michigan like a steam bath. The overpass was also perfect for roosting pigeons, of which there were *a lot*. And where there are a lot of pigeons, there is a lot of pigeon shit.

"I'm just warning you, it's *slick* on the ramps," Greg said, emphasizing "slick" in a way that indicated personal experience with the excrement.

He was there once when the white liquid was like greased lightning. Greg went down and was so repulsed by the marks on his shirt that he opted to toss it in the trash rather than wash it.

But I felt compelled to skate Logan Boulevard anyway, not just for my very scientific research, but to prove something to myself. Though there are surely worse skate parks, I thought if I could skate *here*, I could skate anywhere.

With the exception of the splatters from the pigeons, which, when dry, turned portions of the ramp into miniature Jackson Pollock paintings, the skate park was the kind of gritty I'm familiar with: ramps dotted with stickers and spray paint, a loose screw poking out a little too high, cigarette butts and rocks and leaves on the ground, and coping that is extraordinarily waxed in some places and abruptly dry in others. This skate park didn't frighten me—I knew its kind.

When I dropped in off a bank and zoomed over the hump of tiny pump track, a bump breaking up the monotony of the flat ground, I came over the top and looked down just in time to see a hole in the ramp. The wood had been hacked away by the pounding axes of feet and wheels, leaving a hole big enough to trap my wheels and send me face planting. But I know this grit, this damage, this construction that has taken more abuse than it can stand; I was almost expecting it. At the last moment, I jumped and sailed over the hole to the flat ground, landing safely.

As I traversed the park, I couldn't help noticing the variety of skaters—skateboarders, rollerbladers, and even a few BMXers, along with the ever-present scooter kids; guys in their thirties and forties, as well as tots on skateboards holding onto their mom's hand; white, Black, and Asian folks. I'm reminded of the beautiful mosaic nature of big cities.

I think about the person who told me Chicago didn't have a decent skate park. They were someone I met in passing at an event, and I wish now I'd thought to ask them where they were from, where they normally skated. What was it they were used to? What was it they expected? What made it so difficult for them to skate in this city?

At the end of the day, a janky skate park is better than no skate park, and it's not as if there aren't other skate parks in Chicago. With the crowd of people at Logan Boulevard, I saw the pigeon shit and ramp holes in a new light: this is a well-loved place, I thought. Ramps don't take a beating unless there's someone to skate them, and these ramps have been skated long and hard by devotees, hobbyists, practitioners of the highest order, and folks who are just trying it out.

Greg's warning about Logan Boulevard wasn't unfounded. I would've warned any out-of-towner about it myself. As a lifelong Chicagoan who's been skateboarding since 1985, he knows far better spots and regularly organizes skate meetups.

"During the nineties, I was sponsored and was traveling for skateboarding. I hit that peak," he said, a hint of nostalgia edging his voice. "And the bad part is twenty or thirty years later, when you know where you were, and you go to the skate park and it's all fourteen-year-old kids with a ton of testosterone jumping down stairs. I'm past that age. I'm forty-four, and there are just some things I can't do anymore, like big flights of stairs and handrails."

Recognizing that he may not be able to do all the tricks he used to but that he still had a passion for skateboarding is what inspired him to start Pardon My Thrashing. It began as a Facebook group in 2012 as a way to connect older skateboarders who wanted to meet up for skate sessions and kept growing from there.

"We formed our own crew. Then we found out there are girls who like to skate, but they're scared of the dudes at the skate park. So we were like, 'Hey you can come skate with us. We'll make sure we've got your back,'" Greg said. "It's really not that bad. I think a lot of people worry when they go to a skate park. But whether they're girls or someone who just started or is less experienced, whatever the reason, they get it in their head that the skate park is a scary place and it's not for them, and we want to prove that wrong."

"Skateboarders are probably some of the most welcoming people," Maria added. "Always willing to teach you."

Maria's trajectory is backward compared to most people's. Most people start skating, and then, if they feel inspired to do so, they start a skate-related business. But as Pardon My Thrashing grew from a Facebook page to sponsoring contests to hosting events to getting boards made with their logo to opening a small indoor skate park, Maria was right by Greg's side, helping keep the business going, even though she didn't yet skate herself.

"I started doing stuff because I was there and I love helping. So when his old business partner decided it wasn't for him, it was like, I'm your partner now," she said. "I remember me and my sister [skating] when we were kids, then, I don't know, I got older and it was like, who's going to take care of me if I break my ankle? When you're an adult, you think of all these things."

"Maria was with me there at the Bunker [Pardon My Thrashing's indoor skate park] like every night, even late on weeknights when she had to get up at an obscene time in the morning. She'd stay there late, and we'd have to kick people out at ten, which meant we couldn't get out of there until eleven," Greg added.

"And I had to get up at three-thirty in the morning!" Maria exclaimed. "I work in the suburbs in a hospital. That's what kept me from skateboarding for so long. I'd seen a couple of injuries and it's like, I've got to go to work. If I hurt myself, I won't be able to drive, then how would I get to work? But I got a little jealous of all the people who could do it, so I was like, I gotta get in there."

Maria's story is more relatable than I think she realizes, especially that desire to skate lying dormant for years on end. I knew as a kid in Alabama, being miles and miles away from a skate park, that I desperately wanted to skate one, while also assuming that if I never lived anywhere with a skate park, that desire would just dry up like unwatered grass and go away. But the yearning for wheels under your feet is more like a cicada—able to be buried for a decade-plus and emerge strong and ready as ever. That doesn't mean we love it any less.

Eventually, Maria couldn't fight it.

"Now I get excited when I see my board, like, I can't wait to get on that," she said. "I feel like I've made more friends skateboarding than I did my whole high school career."

That sense of community and finally being able to do something you've wanted to do for years are both things that Karlie Thornton can relate to. Originally from St. Louis, Karlie moved to Chicago for college and eventually made the city her home.

"In middle school, there was this group of boys I was friends with, and they would go to this indoor skate park in the mall called Plan 9. I'd go there and watch them skate all the time after school. I just thought it was so cool. There were never any girls skating, so I just naturally was like, this is a boy's sport, this isn't for girls," Karlie said. "Looking back, I can't believe I thought that."

As an adult, Karlie realized that her experience was part of a wider issue about representation in sports that can affect would-be participants as much as wider public perception.

"When you don't see yourself represented in something, you think this isn't for me until you see someone doing it," she said. "I moved from St. Louis and I bought a skateboard eventually just because I remember from my past thinking it was really cool. I was in a phase of trying new things that I didn't try when I was at home living with my parents. My parents obviously did not want me to be a skateboarder. Like, that's a little boy's sport, that's not for girls. So I was trying things that my parents wouldn't allow me to do."

Even after Karlie started skateboarding, she realized that the representation problem went deeper. Skateboarding, in addition to being predominantly male, is also a very white sport.

"Most of the guys I was around were white and were amazing pro-level skateboarders. And it was like, dang, I would love to see some Black and Brown girls who want to get into skateboarding," she said. "I invited two of my closest friends who I knew kind of liked skateboarding. We just started skating, and more and more people started asking when we were going skating and how they could join us. So it just grew and grew."

That was how froSkate was born in 2019. Like Greg, Karlie took to social media to centralize communications and announce meetups. Now the @froSkate Instagram account has tens of thousands of followers. In addition to skate meetups, froSkate organizes rolling protests around Chicago to defend Black lives—particularly Black trans people who are victims of violence far above the rates for other groups—and defund the police. At their No Brakes protest on July 4, 2020, thousands of people turned out on all kinds of wheels. They continued even as threats of bombing Black Lives Matter protests and of potential mass shootings loomed, even as white supremacists tried to scare them out of raising awareness and agitating for the rights they fully deserve.

"We didn't ask for the police's permission to march because police brutality is an issue in Black communities, and we've seen some instances from all the heavy protests [for George Floyd Jr.] last year. . . . One police officer showed up and was like, 'What are y'all doing? How long is it going to take? We'll let you do this as long as we lead it in the front.' Which was really annoying because we didn't want the police there at all, and we *especially* did not want them leading our protest against the police," Karlie said. "That definitely got on a lot of people's nerves, but if we didn't do that, there would've been violence against us."

For Karlie and the members of froSkate, activism and skating go hand in hand. There's historical precedent for this: Perhaps the most well-known example is Ledger "Roller Man" Smith, who roller skated seven hundred miles to the March on Washington in 1963, where Martin Luther King Jr. delivered his unforgettable "I Have a Dream" speech. While skating through Fort Wayne, Indiana, a man in a car tried to run him over.

One of froSkate's biggest activism goals is to increase access to skate parks in Black, Brown, and immigrant neighborhoods around the city.

"We want people on the South Side and far West Side, where there are fewer skate parks, to skate," she said. "I feel like times are changing where people don't believe Black people skate because, well, look around. The demographic is clearly changing, and it's way more diverse versus years ago where it wasn't like that at all. We've noticed when we're trying to have our meetups that there aren't as many options in the South Side and the far West Side. There's Burnham and there's some West Side skate parks but not really in any Black communities."

A quick look at Google Maps showed me what Karlie already knew. There are clusters of skate parks around the Central, North, and East Sides of the city, but the farther south and west you go, the fewer there are. There are scant few skate parks between Interstate 55 and the Indiana border. Just as it is in St. Louis, the racism of city planning led to resources, opportunity, and access to public spaces being limited by your zip code.

"It's hard for us when we're hosting meetups because we want to be skating with these communities, but there are no skate parks there. So unless you're willing and can find a way to take a long trek to Wilson Skate Park up north or if you can get a ride to Clemente [Roberto Clemente High School] or Grant . . . there's a long way to go in terms of diversifying skate parks around the city," Karlie said.

Thanks to froSkate's donors, if people are having trouble getting to meetups, they can DM the group on Instagram to arrange transportation. Until skate parks are democratized across the Windy City, froSkate is doing what they can to level the playing field. This is particularly challenging in winter, when the outdoor skate parks are unusable, there are few indoor skate parks around the city in general, and the privately owned indoor parks charge for entry. Though it's a massive undertaking, Karlie is looking into what it would take to open an indoor skate park in the communities she most wants to see able to skate.

"You have to drive like forty minutes to find an indoor spot here," she said. "When you talk about the logistics—and I've spoken to the folks at Fargo Skate [in DeKalb, Illinois, about an hour and a half from the lakeshore] and Four Seasons [in Milwaukee] about their experiences—there's a reason there aren't many indoor parks in Chicago. The city does not make it easy at all," Karlie said, sighing. "There are a lot of factors you have to consider, and insurance and permitting are two of the biggest. Everyone is scared that a skateboarder is going to get hurt and sue, so no one really wants to help out with stuff like that."

And that's not even mentioning Chicago's rent. For the kind of multi-thousand-square-foot space you'd need to build an indoor skate park inside city limits, the rent would be exorbitant.

Greg and Maria know firsthand how challenging it can be to run even a small indoor skate spot in the city.

"For Chicago indoor skate parks, there's Asylum up north, Audubon Skate Park in Elk Grove, and the Den and Fargo are way out in the western suburbs, which are both owned by women. . . . There's a House of Vans, but it was always more of an entertainment venue with a skate park in it, and they'd open up randomly. You had to sign up online to get in; you couldn't just show up. It was more confusing than anything, so I don't think people ever really considered it a skate park," Greg said. "Then there was the Bunker, and we were only around for a year."

Greg and Maria started the Bunker because they needed office space and storage space for Pardon My Thrashing's goods. They'd started designing their own boards, as well as other merch like stickers, koozies, and shirts. They needed a space to pack and ship, as well as to edit videos and plan events. The spot they found had been a private DIY built by a roller skater who then wanted to travel and needed someone to take over the space. Even though Pardon My Thrashing had to borrow some ramps and build new ones, the spot was ideal—way better than typical storage and office space.

Then the coronavirus hit.

The pandemic had a strange effect on Pardon My Thrashing. As the need for outdoor activities rose, skateboard sales surged even as raw materials were harder to come by. At the same time, Greg and Maria weren't able to keep the Bunker open due to the city's lockdown rules. Businesses that chose to defy the shutdown order and remain open risked losing their business licenses, and if Pardon My Thrashing lost their business license, they wouldn't be able to sell skateboards. Not knowing how long the coronavirus would ravage the world, they opted not to renew their lease when it came up.

"We needed to move out and move on," Greg said. "We weren't going to open another spot during COVID, and even now, we're still hesitant until this is far beyond us. Meanwhile, there are so many more people skating, and we can barely keep up with the skateboarding side of the business. We came real close to running out of boards."

"It was sad, but it had to be done," Maria added.

With the Bunker closed, Pardon My Thrashing's goal was to promote the indoor skate parks in the region when they were able to open at a reduced capacity.

"For those skate parks, that's their main business. For us, we're a skateboard company, so the skate park was just this added bonus. We wanted to make sure those other spots stuck around through COVID," Greg said. "It was a scary time. We did as much as we could to help keep them around."

Between the barriers to starting an indoor skate park, the challenge of keeping indoor skate parks open through the pandemic, and the general lack of skate parks throughout Chicago's Black communities, I can't help thinking again of Logan Boulevard Skate Park with its grit and grime. Being under an overpass, it's likely the closest thing to a free, public indoor skate park in Chicago's city limits. It makes sense to me why so many different people chose to skate that park, and I imagine the diversity only increases as the temperature drops, at least to the point when not even the hardiest Chicagoans want to be outdoors.

Even in a skate scene as vast as the Windy City's, people like Greg, Maria, and Karlie are hosting skate events that increase access and a sense of welcome for skaters of all ages, races, ethnicities, income levels, wheels, and skill levels. They do as much as they can within the confines that capitalism and the government have set forth to build strong communities around skating.

"The scene in Chicago is vast. People and groups represent all the niches of skateboarding. Whether you go to a skate park and think, I might feel intimidated or I'm not sure if I should be around these people, know that everyone here is super cool and welcoming," said Greg. "When you go to a skate park, you're going to make new friends."

"I think the scene in Chicago is progressing beautifully. I just want us to continue to grow in diversity," Karlie said. "I want there to be more femme people and queer people and more BIPOC folks working at skate shops. I want to see us showing up more at the skate parks, even alone, and feeling comfortable. I want more nontraditional skaters to get invited to private skate sessions. We're moving toward the right direction for sure."

What they've created and continue to create is better than decent—it's an important, necessary change in a city that has room for all skaters but so often doesn't provide the infrastructure. To whom do public skate parks belong? Who, in the grand scheme of the city, is supported in their desire to skate?

In the meantime, there's always Logan Boulevard. In his Google review, Andrés says simply, "Decent skate park," and I can't help but agree.

Northeastern Illinois and Northwestern Indiana

CHICAGOLAND

Travel thirty minutes outside Chicago, and it's easy to forget just how massive the city is, just how Tetris-ed together the city's pieces are. The space where urban sprawl turns into the suburbs turns into the country looks universal: the gradual spreading out, the stripes of strip malls along the interstate, the clusters of chain restaurants until you go so far there are seldom any chain restaurants at all. You could be anywhere; you could be in the middle of everywhere.

Borders are so often arbitrary, invisible boundaries of separation created without good cause. They usually create an unnecessary "us versus them" dichotomy. Nonetheless, in interviewing people in and around Chicago, the concerns of skaters inside the city felt different than the concerns of those outside it. Though these skaters didn't seem to disdain the city itself, they'd all deliberately chosen not to live there and preferred to do most of their skating closer to home—whether that was southwest of the city or southeast into northwest Indiana.

The idea that skating is only an urban sport, unheard of in more rural areas, is wrong. And it's been wrong for a long time. Ariel Ries, the owner of Fargo Skateboarding; Ikeem Jones (skate name Keemo Supremo), the owner of Royal Skate and Apparel; and Gerald J. Schleitwiler (skate name

Gnarly Jargon), who's worked at half a dozen skate shops and is known for sailing down some of the longest rails around, all do their work in the skate world in the southern Chicagoland area.

In the same way that indie bookstores are vital to the fabric of the literary community, independently owned and operated skate shops are crucial to the skate community. In addition to selling the goods that make the sport possible, they often host or sponsor events such as film screenings, clinics with pros, contests, and more. They're a major artery to the skate community, providing lifeblood. It's work that's becoming increasingly difficult to sustain as online retail continues to grow and specialty shops can't compete in the race-to-the-bottom pricing that big-box stores thrive on.

Long before she was a skate shop owner, Ariel was destined to be a skater.

"My grandma was a professional roller skater, doing the waltz and the foxtrot, the ballroom style. She roller skated six or seven days a week until she was seventy-three years old," Ariel said. "That was a really big influence on me. I'd go skating at the roller rink every Sunday night with her when I was a kid."

It wasn't until Ariel was in eighth grade that she found the wheels that called to her. She and her best friend found two skateboards in her friend's basement: one was a banana-board style from the late seventies, and the other was a big cruiser style from the eighties. Ariel claimed the cruiser.

"We took those boards all over town and to other towns. We really fell in love with going down hills and going fast and using it to be away from the house all day. Skateboarding was our escape, a way to feel freedom," she said. "We both had parents who were alcoholics, so the skateboard was our vehicle to get away from that life."

When Ariel and her best friend were high school freshmen in the small town of Kingston, Illinois, they finally got newer skateboards that had the kind of agility required for shredding a skate park. They were so excited, although not everyone in the skate park shared their enthusiasm.

"This boy took my skateboard and ran into the woods, where he took a big fat shit on it. He shit on my skateboard! It was the bottom of the board where the trucks and wheels are, so he shit right on the center of the board, and all his friends are laughing so hard. Then he flipped it over in the grass and broke it in half after shitting on it. I had to walk home. It was devastating," Ariel said. "I did get another skateboard, but that messed with me at that age. I lost confidence."

The pull toward the board was too strong to keep her away for long. While in college, Ariel met a skateboarder who was a decade older than she was who'd owned a skate shop for a few years in the late 1990s and early 2000s. He lost the shop and made it his mission to get another one. After they started dating, he and Ariel opened a shop together in DeKalb in 2007. Ariel was just a junior in college.

She started skateboarding more, remembering why she fell in love with it in the first place, and her boyfriend sold her on the idea of an indoor skate park. She loved the idea, but their relationship was rocky— she said he was abusive and that he cheated on her. They decided to break up while still continuing to move forward with the skate park.

They signed a lease on an eighteen-thousand-square-foot warehouse in Schaumberg, Illinois, and tried to get it built as quickly as possible. But one thing after another happened. Ariel was getting so many signs from the universe that the cosmos was practically screaming that this was a bad idea.

"It was things like zoning and permitting, the landlord saying it was zoned for commercial use and assembly but it was actually zoned for manufacturing," Ariel sighed. "It failed before we even got it open to the public. It was horrible."

Though the skate park didn't work out, they kept the skate shop and continued working together.

"I kept telling myself it's fine, it's fine," Ariel said, recalling those years when she tried to convince herself, but everything changed on her twenty-ninth birthday.

"We were about to sign the lease on what I have now, which is the Fargo Theater, a ten-thousand-square-foot theater space that was built in 1929 that I turned into a skate park. I woke up at 6:30 in the morning and my dad said to me, 'Hey, don't sign the lease with that guy. It's not going to work out. If you do it by yourself, you'll be fine, but do *not* do it with him. It's not going to work,'" Ariel said.

She was taken aback by her dad's insistence until her best friend confirmed it. "She was like, 'Yeah, can you imagine doing all the work *without* him yelling at you and telling you what to do? You do it all anyway, so it'd be minus him yelling at you and taking all the cash.'"

On that day, Ariel changed the passwords on everything, changed the locks to the skate shop, and added up the inventory and saw its value. When her ex-boyfriend came in that day, shocked at the change, she told him, "I'm buying you out, and you don't get a choice. This is a long time coming, and it's either you or me, and everything is already in my name."

In his devastation, she said he tried to sabotage the shop and blackmail her. She ended up paying him $1,500 a month for a year to move on, and she signed the lease on the Fargo Theater by herself. She convinced some friends to help build the ramps, and with the help of the local small business development center, the skate park opened to the public five years ago, a fitting companion to the skate shop that had been open for fourteen years.

With shutdown orders in effect and strict rules on capacity, I was curious to know how Ariel fared during the pandemic.

"COVID was actually one of the biggest blessings for us because we were able to shut down and qualify for business loans to work on the ramps. We took that and tore down the entire park and rebuilt it every single day. That was huge because it was kind of just pieced together. There was never a time where we could rip the whole thing down and start from scratch. It was a huge thing for us, and it really paid off," she said. "With the timing, I can't even believe it. If we'd decided to do that this year . . . the price of materials, like wood, has quadrupled. The way it came together, I feel so lucky."

Ariel's dad was right: if she built Fargo Skateboarding herself, it would work out.

Southeast of DeKalb in Lansing, Illinois, the pandemic did a number on Keemo Supremo's shop, Royal Skate and Apparel. He opened the brick-and-mortar shop in 2013 and had a small online presence, preferring to focus on the physical location, but the coronavirus forced him to close the doors and move to selling online only. The switch came with a steep learning curve, though Keemo stayed positive.

"It sucks, but it silver-lining sucks," he explained. "Because at the time we were right out of winter, and when winter hits for a skate shop, you're not making any money. It's just going to be slow, and you're going to be losing a lot of money. So we were right out of winter and then it's March, it's COVID. Since we had to shut down the [physical] store, we can focus our money on products and throwing events. We're getting in position to get Royal products in stores everywhere. So, silver lining," he added, shrugging.

Keemo grew up in Roseland, a neighborhood on Chicago's South Side, around 104th Street.

"It's the middle of the hood," he said. "There was no skateboarding over there, really. No skate parks and not really any skateboarders."

Then one day, he saw a kid doing kickflips off a curb and he was entranced. That inspired him to watch the X Games, where skateboarders shred gigantic ramps, often airing out over the top of the ramp, suspended in the air for seconds on end.

"It was just mind-blowing. Like, whoa, what the hell are you doing? I'm like, this dude can fucking fly?! I want to fly one day! From that point on, I identified as a skater," Keemo said.

That was before he got his own skateboard. ("Nobody is giving me a skateboard—I'm in Roseland," he said.) In the meantime, he got a piece of wood with no wheels and would flip it around with his feet and land on it. He didn't get a real skateboard until he was fourteen.

Keemo has been skateboarding for fifteen years now, over half his life. Looking back on it, that one kid doing kickflips was the only kid he ever saw in the neighborhood doing any kind of tricks, or doing anything different than the little kids who rode down hills on their knees and butts. The kickflip kid is like an apparition, a sign Keemo was meant to see.

His family fell on hard times when Keemo was thirteen, and Keemo, his mom, and two brothers moved in with an uncle. They had to sleep on the floor. When his aunt announced she had bought a house in Burnham, Illinois, half an hour south of the city and close to Lansing, she invited them to move in with her.

"It was so different from the city to here. Real culture shock. I've been on both sides, and when I moved here, it was like the Disney Channel," he said, laughing. "Things are more spread out. I can hear crickets. I love being able to go to the city and know my way around, then come back and it be quiet. I don't have to hear ambulances all day."

It turns out that having more space and more peace of mind gave Keemo the environment he needed to become the skater he wanted to be.

"I moved to the burbs and started seeing skateboarding," Keemo said, remembering how excited he was. "It was like, oh shit, I'm not the only one! I made friends with some skateboarders, and we'd skate every day. AriZona [Iced Tea] and honey buns were my diet. Go back and do it all again the next day."

Keemo knew early on that he wanted to have a skate business. His mom was an entrepreneur and had her own hair salon, so he saw from a young age that if you're good at something, you might as well learn how to make a living at it. Before Royal, when he was twenty-two, he had a business where he bought blank skateboards, then he and his friends would paint them and sell them as works of art. Not long after that, he and a friend/business partner who worked on the skateboard art decided they wanted to open a storefront. They found a space, and the landlord even gave them a few months rent-free to open.

"The first day was awesome, a ton of skaters were there. Then after that, everyone was like, we bought all our shit already. So we go three or four months with barely any money coming in during our first year, and we're like, oh my god, we're losing all this money," he said.

One by one, his business partner and employees dropped off, but Keemo kept going. He held onto the store for seven years until the pandemic sealed the retail location's fate.

Even though I could tell he missed having a storefront, Keemo's optimism about the future is infectious. He's bubbly and animated, even though he describes himself as shy and has a self-deprecating sense of humor, smiling as he ragged on himself for not being the best skater. He laughs and you can't help laughing with him, even when he's being vulnerable about the challenges of trying to run one of the few Black-owned skate shops in the region. He may not always take himself seriously, but he takes skateboarding very seriously.

In doing so, Keemo saw the connection between skateboarding and art, especially music. In the vein of skate shops being community hubs for skaters, Keemo recognized the crossover between skateboarders and musicians and used the store as a venue.

"We'd throw parties and do big music events, like hardcore and techno. It was a crazy time. There'd be hundreds of people coming in and out," Keemo said.

It was through having shows at the shop that Keemo connected with Gnarly Jargon, who raps and skateboards.

"I did a hip-hop show with skateboarders who rap. It's a big thing, skateboarders who rap and guys who rap who skateboard too. We called it a skrapper show," Gnarly said. "Royal was one of the biggest venues/skate shops that was ever around in our area, so it was super fun. We [Gnarly and Keemo] solidified our friendship through five years of doing shows."

Though Gnarly is still involved with the online business side of Royal, the old storefront will forever hold a nostalgic place in his heart.

"Maybe my second or third year in with Royal, I was still dating the woman who is now my wife. I'd been dating her for two years, and I actually proposed to her inside of Royal," Gnarly said. "Then we turned this private indoor skate park called the BZHQ, that's not there anymore, into a wedding venue. So I proposed to my girlfriend in a skate shop and I got married in a skate park. I'm living my best life as a skateboarder."

Even before Royal, Gnarly Jargon was no stranger to skate shops. His very first job in the summer after he graduated high school was at No Comply Skate Shop in Whiting, Indiana, in the early 2000s. He clicked with the owner, and she hired him on the spot the first time he stepped into the shop.

"I was there from 2002 to 2004. After that, I went skate shop to skate shop because each one went out of business," Gnarly said with a sigh. "It's almost the natural order of things because skateboarding is just not a lucrative thing. You get a bubble here and a recession here, bad management there. It was come and go."

In the mid-2000s, Gnarly worked at Woodland Skates in Portage, Indiana. When the owner, Jason, heard that No Comply had shut down, he immediately hired Gnarly. Woodland was one of the best skate shops in the area and not just because there was a skate park across the street.

"Jason hired me to run his eBay store. I was selling hundreds of boards and grip tape every single day. He sold completes [skateboards with the trucks and wheels already mounted, as opposed to individual parts to be assembled for a custom build] on eBay, and it was really lucrative," Gnarly said, thinking back to how novel online shopping was at the time. "I remember he bought like $30,000 worth of one item and we sold it out within a year."

The shop was doing well, though Gnarly left to be closer to his then girlfriend, who lived in Whiting, Indiana.

"It was too far of a drive, like forty minutes, and it was just not working out, so I quit. I shouldn't have; it was the best job I've ever had," he said.

Word spread about his experience in skate shops, and it didn't take him long to find another job at Old Town Skates in Whiting. The shop came first, then the city built a skate park nearby, which was exciting because they hoped the shop's proximity to the skate park would drive foot traffic to the shop. Gnarly enthusiastically joined the committee to get that skate park built, but the city ignored the local skaters' suggestions about what the community wanted.

"All of us on the committee were street skaters, so we skated stairs, rails, and ledges and weren't doing vert stuff. We told the city officials that, and they said they were listening to us, but these Chicago guys came in and said they should build a big half-pipe and bowl. They wanted something for skaters who really want to carve around and do aerials like Tony Hawk," Gnarly explained. "They really sold the idea to the committee, and all of us street skaters got ignored."

The choice to make the skate park more ramps, bowls, and vert had a huge impact on sales at Old Town Skates. The business of skateboarding is that street skaters break their boards more often than vert skaters due to the impact of jumping and landing on the board that grinding rails and sailing over stairs requires. Thus, street skaters spend more money at skate shops replacing their gear than skaters who only carve bowls and half-pipes.

"The skate park ended up being super cool for the touristy thing—like, guys from Chicago would come skate, but they'd never support the shop nearby. All our local skaters wouldn't go through boards as much because the park forced them to skate vert, so business kind of fizzled," Gnarly said. "People would buy one board a year and ride it the whole year."

Old Town Skates suffered a couple of bad years before closing, and those years were a dark time for Gnarly Jargon. His car got stolen, then he and his then girlfriend broke up and she kicked him out of her house, so he was unhoused for a while and had to live in the shop.

"I almost committed suicide at that point, but I had a moment in that time where I wanted to turn my life around," Gnarly said. "I Russian Rouletted the Bible, and I opened it to Job. The story of Job is that he lost everything. God was testing him, and I thought, that's a lot like me right now. I had a feeling of God speaking to me, saying, 'You're here for a purpose, go find it. Go find what you're meant to do,' and it was like, it's skateboarding. I decided, no, I'm not going to end it now—instead, I'm going to go try this trick."

That's when he decided to try grinding what locals call the EC13 rail. It's a handrail over thirteen stairs at an East Chicago, Indiana, high school, and it's the biggest rail in the area. It's the kind of rail that only pros would have the skills to do successfully. As deadly as the EC13 might be for most, skating it kept Gnarly alive.

"I figured I'll do the scariest thing ever. I'm going to skate a big rail, and, well, if I die, I may as well get knocked out skateboarding. That was my mentality," he said. "Then I landed it, so it was like, I didn't die, so I guess I have to find another rail."

Gnarly's favorite things to skate are rails, and it's where his skills truly shine. He first learned to boardslide by tipping over a freestanding basketball hoop that he propped up on cinder blocks. Later, after he proposed to his girlfriend, Sonya, inside Royal, he got the itch to do the Dyer Twelve, a twelve-stair handrail at the skate park in Dyer, Indiana, that's even bigger and steeper than the EC13. But by then he was no longer suicidal and had something to lose.

"I was scared to do it. I was risking breaking something right before the wedding," he said. "When I told Sonya I was doing the big rail like a week or two before the wedding, she was like, 'Well, make sure you have a good haircut for the video.' She's the biggest supporter of my life. It's like jumping off a small house onto your face, and I pulled it off."

After Old Town closed, Gnarly worked some nonskate jobs before finding Tyrant Skate Shop in Hammond, Indiana, in 2010—also unfortunately short-lived—and then Royal in 2013. Talking to Gnarly is like getting a history lesson in Chicago's suburban skate shops, and while some might think it futile to go from one skate shop to another after seeing so many go out of business over the years, I was instead struck by the resilience of Gnarly Jargon and the shop owners. They each knew the odds stacked against them and chose to go for their dreams anyway. Talk to any skater and they'll tell you that skating teaches persistence and resiliency—the only way to get good is to do the same tricks over and over, consistently practicing—but I didn't realize how much those characteristics carried over into the skate ecosystem in general.

And I can't help lamenting how, even with so much resilience, the odds are so stacked against skate shops to the point that at least half a dozen in south Chicagoland alone have been lost in the past twenty years. I think about how much Fargo Skateboarding does for the community and how much stronger skating communities everywhere would be if they had skate shops like it.

"I wanted an event space so we could do things like a class on making jewelry from broken skateboards. My boyfriend is a filmer, so he did a class on how to film and edit skateboard videos. We've had paint-a-skateboard sessions, you name it," Ariel said.

Having a space can also mean making that space welcome to people who have been historically marginalized and ostracized by the skate community.

"We get people of all ages, and I try to accommodate different types of people so they feel more welcome. We do a thirty-and-older skate time, a ladies' night, and an LGBTQ night. We have a time just for beginners and beginner sessions where we skate alongside the beginners and give them pointers. I'm trying to be inviting to the skaters who wouldn't necessarily come to the shop and park because they might not feel like it's a place for them," Ariel said. "Just being a woman-owned place, I do think that we do attract more women and femme vibes."

As she told me this, I recalled the story of the boy who took a shit on her skateboard before breaking it, and I thought how, so often, skate shop owners give to the community what they themselves need and didn't have when they were younger.

"I gave away my favorite skateboard," Keemo said. "I was walking and I saw a little girl in the alley and she was on a Walmart board. And I know what Walmart boards feel like: it's awful. She was trying to ollie and turn around on it and I said, 'Let me see your board.' She showed it to me and I said, 'This is not gonna work.' So I gave her my board. I was like, I'll get another one, I own a store."

I recall him telling me about his struggle to get a skateboard when he was younger, flipping a plank of wood around with his feet for years until someone gave him their old board. Keemo was paying it forward, coming full circle. And maybe within the next decade, there'll be a girl on the US skateboarding team giving an interview about how some guy in an alley gave her his skateboard and changed her life. Though perhaps cheesy and sentimental, I allow myself this dream because a skateboard is a dream made manifest, and the Chicagoland skate scene wouldn't be what it is without its dreamers.

Having a shop is what allowed him to give away his board without worry, and it's what allows Ariel to give back to local kids through her nonprofit, Pushing Together.

"In DeKalb [County], 60 percent of people under eighteen are living below the poverty level. That's a high percentage, and there are a lot of young people here. We did some math and learned that 10 percent of kids want to skateboard, which means there are at least four hundred kids in our town who don't have the means to skateboard," Ariel explained. "So we're trying to do an initiative called Skateboarding for Everybody to introduce everyone in our town to skateboarding as a way of identifying the four hundred kids who want to skateboard and can't afford it so we can provide them with skateboards, shoes, equipment, and access to the indoor skate park."

I couldn't help considering how things might have been different for Keemo if there'd been a skate shop near him growing up on Chicago's

South Side and if there'd been an initiative like this. To dwell on the past and its could've beens and should've beens is an exercise in futility—all we can do now is to support the skate shops we have.

"Too many skaters want stuff for free, and they need to support their local skate shops by buying from them. You got to support the people who support you," Gnarly Jargon said.

The future of Royal is uncertain. Though Keemo Supremo is selling goods online and is enthusiastic about getting his wares in retail skate shops around the region, I think of what has disappeared with the loss of this Black-owned, brick-and-mortar skate shop.

"There was something more tangible about being able to interact with the people. There was a vibe. People started to gravitate toward us because of our personality, and you lose a lot of that online. You get someone who needs a skateboard and it becomes who's selling a board for the cheapest? Instead of, 'I want to support these people because these people are cool,'" Keemo said. "If I have a board and Amazon has that board for ten dollars cheaper, it's like fuck you, they're going to Amazon. But I'm a person and I'm going to use this money to live."

I was a writer long before I was a skater, and I was a voracious reader long before I was a writer. I've seen what happens when the literary community rallies around its indie bookstores, when bookstore devotees eschew Amazon and choose to spend their dollars with local booksellers. The booksellers who recommend books from the heart, not an algorithm; who organize book clubs and book signings with beloved authors; who create safe spaces in their communities for vulnerable populations. I've also seen what happens when those indie bookstores are forced to shut their doors and how neighborhoods with book deserts suffer. Hundreds of bookstores closed in the years Amazon rose to power, and more were lost in the wake of the Great Recession, and though it's taken over a decade, they're bouncing back. It was a long time coming, but the literary community came to its collective senses and realized that there are more important things than rock-bottom deals. Some things are priceless. The skating community is long overdue for such a reckoning.

When I asked Keemo Supremo what he wants people to know, he said, "Everybody who wants to skateboard, just keep pushing. That's all that matters. Keep pushing and smile while you do it."

For all of our sakes, I hope he and all the other skate shop owners take his advice.

Detroit, Michigan

SKATER HOUSES

Detroit is a city made for skaters. It is the home of the RollerCade, the oldest Black-owned roller rink in the country, which has been operated by the same family since 1955. It's also the home of Detroit-style skating, a synchronized couples skate. It's a city that was made by and for those who roll. And that's without even mentioning cars.

The city's skate scene can be depicted, too, without harping on its infrastructure. Much has been written about the Motor City's empty buildings, with laments for the city often manifesting as poverty porn or like a script for an apocalyptic movie. Too many hipsters have gone with camera in hand in search of beauty in the destruction in the name of creating art that so depersonalizes the destruction from the people whose lives are most affected by it. But there is much more to Detroit than this. In terms of street skating, empty buildings and unmonitored, unguarded private property are the stuff of dreams, and skaters here, like skaters anywhere, make use of what they have. I myself was born in a city of broken concrete, jagged, bent handrails, unmown grass, and abandoned factories whose tenants had moved overseas, leaving behind husks of buildings, empty and wanting. My dad worked at a steel mill for thirty-two years until the day its doors permanently closed, and I refuse to pretend there's a silver lining in deindustrialization and the poverty that comes with it.

All this is to say, I went to Detroit in search of new stories.

I drove miles of winding roads past glittering lakes to arrive at Dan Mancina's house. His five-month-old Newfoundland puppy greeted me with a howl and bounded to a hole he'd exuberantly been digging.

"Not much of a seeing-eye dog," Dan joked as he pushed dirt back into the hole and tamped it down.

Dan had only recently gotten back from competing at Dew Tour in Des Moines, where he'd mentioned that the street course, at least where the competition was held, wasn't accessible for blind and low-vision skaters. Dan was diagnosed with Retinitis pigmentosa, a rare degenerative eye disease, as a teenager and was slowly losing his vision until about three years ago, when he became completely blind.

It was when he was a teenager, too, that he fell in love with skateboarding.

"I was snowboarding a lot, and I read an article in a snowboard magazine that said if you skateboard in the summer, it can keep you on point. So I started skateboarding a bit and learning about tricks. Then I met a group of friends who skated, and that's when it took over," Dan said.

By the end of middle school, he was hooked. They didn't start building skate parks around Livonia, the Detroit suburb where Dan grew up, until he was in high school, so Dan and his friends were all street skaters.

"We skated the local Kmart ledges, and the high school had all the stairs. Then we started riding our bikes going farther and farther," Dan said.

Eventually, Dan went about as far as you can go: moving to California to skate. For so many skaters, that's the dream—but he found that SoCal wasn't as great as he'd been led to believe.

"They built the big Venice Beach skate park while I was there, and I remember this whole squad of dudes who were hanging onto that old-school vibe. Older guys and surfers who were hardcore scary dudes who would come up and act like they owned the park. Like, 'We got this park built, we own the park.' It was a weird vibe," Dan said.

Aside from the unnecessarily threatening attitude of ownership over the park, Dan found Southern California strange precisely because he had the perspective that skating in the Midwest had given him.

"I was like, you got a park built in Venice Beach, California, the mecca of skateboarding, and I did the same stuff and got a park built in Livonia, Michigan. What are you even talking about? Skate parks out there are a dime a dozen," he said.

After a couple of years in Southern California, during which time he had a son and decided he wanted to go back to school, he moved back to Michigan. The time out West left him disillusioned with the sport he loved.

"I didn't even skate at that point," he said. "I was over skateboarding. I was over the whole scene. LA was way different than the Midwest skate scene, and I wasn't really feeling it. It was just not what I thought it would be. It was super cliquey."

That, combined with his deteriorating vision, made him think he was done with skateboarding for good. There was a two-year period where he had no drive to skate at all. It was a dark, depressing time.

There's something about skating that's almost encoded into skaters' DNA. If you have the inclination to skate, you won't be able to stay away from it. There's an instinctual pull that won't let you avoid the adrenaline rush of wheels under your feet for too long.

"I'm way happier and I'm a better person when I'm on my board," he said.

When Dan picked up a skateboard again, he was more determined than ever. He started making a series of videos to challenge the public's assumptions about what blind people are capable of, and he started filming himself skateboarding. The videos took off on Instagram.

"It was weird having people call me inspirational at first. It's still a little weird," Dan said, chuckling. "I'm just a skater. I don't see myself as inspirational, but it feels good to know people enjoy watching my skating. And the bonus is that people are inspired by it, especially those who are visually impaired or just found out they're going blind. It's cool to hear from them."

Dan is still primarily a street skater and will skate any accessible place, especially if there's a good ledge, round bar, or flat rail. He enjoys going around and finding new spots, though he doesn't often find them at skate parks because accessibility is almost always left out of the design process.

When Dan goes to a skate park, he has a process of walking the park to figure out what he can skate. More often than not, the obstacles are too small. Because Dan skateboards with his white cane, he has to be able to locate the obstacle and get a sense of its height and length before he can skate it.

"If a ledge is tiny and only eight feet long, then by the time I find it, I'm already past it, especially if I've got any kind of speed," he explained.

That's why Dan started his nonprofit, Keep Pushing. He's working toward building an accessible skate park right in his own backyard, where he can invite blind and low-vision people, especially kids, to skate.

"It's all about the size of the obstacles. They have to be really long so you have time to find them, whether it's a ledge or rail. Or if it's a manual pad, it's got to be really wide, with a lot of room for error. Quarter-pipes need to be like fifty feet wide," said Dan. "Most people who are visually impaired have some residual vision, so having good contrast is important, like where the ground is a light color and the obstacle is a dark color. And using auditory cues and lights within obstacles to help guide you to it and let you know where the edges or where the end or the middle of an obstacle is. And textured ground to let you know when you're getting close to a dangerous area."

The program would also incorporate Vision Rehab Teaching, or VRT, which teaches blind and low-vision people the skills they need to live independently, including how to use a white cane. Dan went to grad school at Western Michigan University, one of the best universities in the world for VRT.

Real Skateboards, a brand Dan has used since he was a kid, surprised him with his own pro board a couple of years ago, complete with raised Braille and a nose indicator that helps skaters easily identify the parts of the board. The board's first release sold out—a good sign for the increased awareness around accessibility in skateboarding—so Real is doing another run.

Building a skate park is an expensive undertaking in general, and because larger obstacles often require more money to build, creating an adaptive skate park is especially costly. Dan is relying on donations to Keep Pushing and the proceeds of his pro board to help fund the accessible skate park.

Unfortunately, funding isn't the only barrier to bringing the adaptive skate park to life.

"It has to do with zoning," Dan sighed. "I'm not allowed to build certain things. The city government is a pain in the ass. I have a design that's ready to go. I just need help figuring out the zoning and exactly how big of a structure I can build."

When Dan gestured to his backyard, the site of the future adaptive skate park, I could see it in my mind's eye. He's already got two long rails back there, and more recently, he also got a long manual pad with a quarter-pipe on the end made by Keen Ramps. Dan's sight may be gone, but his vision for helping others and changing lives through skateboarding is clearer than ever.

I can't help imagining an alternative history, one where Dan was so dismayed at the skate scene in California, purportedly the greatest in the world, that he stopped skateboarding altogether. I think about all the people who would have never heard of him or seen his videos, all the people who wouldn't know skateboarding as a blind person was not only possible but also professionally and financially rewarding. Dan's full-time job is being a professional skateboarder, doing what he loves, and he's able to make a difference. He's currently working with skaters and designers in Florida to build the first full-size, public, accessible skate park.

I'm in awe of Dan's street skating, and not just because he's blind or because he's damn good at it. Though every skate park is different, there's a certain predictability to them. You can reasonably assume the surfaces will be smooth; a quarter-pipe is a quarter-pipe, a manual pad is a manual pad. I'm comforted by the certainty of even the jankiest of skate parks, and I realize more than ever that as an able-bodied person, that's a real privilege. There's no such predictability in street skating. Dan has to be quick on his feet to skate like he does.

Sepi Shokri also wants to make the world a better place through skating. When I arrived at her house, her bluetick hound greeted me with a hearty, nose-to-the-sky howl. Sepi offered me a steaming cup of Persian tea, its spices a balm against the heavy summer rain, and I considered how the skaters of Detroit were the only ones who had invited me to their homes. When skaters speak of meeting up with folks in the local skate scene of a new city they're visiting and immediately feeling like family, I understand what they mean.

The rain didn't dampen our ability to skate. Sepi has a mini-ramp in her garage, a practice ramp about two feet tall that's perfect for learning new tricks before taking your newly acquired skills to something bigger.

"I feel like I've got a little piece of the Shred Shed here with me," she said.

Sepi moved to Detroit from Madison, Wisconsin, where she was instrumental in bringing the Shred Shed to life. She still pays for a key and manages the rent from afar. It was hard for her to leave—Sepi grew up in Southern California and moved to Appleton, Wisconsin, for college and ended up making the state her home for twelve years—but when two of her best friends moved to Ann Arbor, it just wasn't the same without them.

Like Melissa and Natsuko, Sepi came to park skating by way of roller derby, though her retirement from derby wasn't voluntary and had nothing to do with the pandemic.

In January 2018, Sepi was at the top of her roller derby game and had gone to Manchester, England, to compete in the World Cup, representing Iran. Coming off of that high, she played in the Clover Cup in Dallas that March, where her team was vying for first place.

"I hit this skater out of bounds and we both ate shit. I was laughing because it was like, that was ridiculous. I hit this person, they went flying, I went flying, and I took us both out of game play. It was zero-sum and didn't help the game at all," she said. "I think the skater thought I was laughing *at* them because a couple of jams later, this person was not with the rest of the team. It didn't make sense where they were positioned. They were facing me and I was like, they're about to fuck me up."

That skater hit Sepi counterclockwise in the jaw.

"My jaw still clicks," she said, demonstrating. I could hear the clicking even though I was sitting across a table from her. "That's permanent. I had a life-altering brain injury from the concussion. My eyes were processing things at different times because you could see how one eye would focus and then the other eye would focus. That's probably what was causing my headaches and the tension in my neck. I didn't have symptom-free days for five months."

She tried massage, acupuncture, sports medicine, and physical therapy—anything to heal and get back to skating. Though her doctor discouraged her from playing derby anytime soon, he said that if there was another way she could skate, then she should do it as part of her physical therapy. She was instructed to get her heart rate up and stop when she felt dizzy or started to have other symptoms.

Though she'd tried park skating a handful of times previously—she hadn't had much time for it because of her commitment to derby—it became her primary mode of skating after her injury.

"With park skating, I have total control over how much I skate and my progress. You don't have the pressure of the derby bouts," she said.

Sepi made it a goal to skate every day that August as part of her healing, and it helped, so she wanted to keep going. It was the realization that winter might impede her healing progress that made her want to start the Shred Shed. And when she decided to move to Detroit, Sepi chose her neighborhood based on its proximity to an indoor skate park.

Detroit has skate parks aplenty, though Sepi has avoided getting involved with the skate community here in the way she did in Madison— and not just because of COVID and a desire to social distance.

"I was really overwhelmed in Madison. For a while, people would be upset if I didn't tell them I was going to the skate park, or five people would say, 'Text me next time you're going.' But I can't let every single person know every time I'm going," Sepi said. "For quite a while, people would come one or two times and I'd teach them stuff, then they'd never come back. So I was teaching people constantly how to pump, how to drop in. I'd basically go to a park and feel guilty if I didn't help people learn."

I thought of all the times I'd seen someone do a trick I'd been wanting to nail and asked for tips. There's a pressure to being a good skater and leader in the skate community that I didn't realize because, frankly, I'm not that good.

Sepi has a big heart and works to make a difference in the skating community, though her burnout with people's demands on her in Madison wasn't the first time she'd been pushed to her wit's end by her fellow skaters. She started the BIPOC Who Skate Instagram account to highlight diversity in roller skating.

"I was really frustrated because, at the time, it was just Moxi and CIB [Community In Bowls, which had only recently changed its name from Chicks In Bowls after demands for gender inclusivity], and every other person on those pages was white, skinny, cisgender, and doing pie-in-the-sky backflips," Sepi said. "I wanted to create a page highlighting BIPOC skaters, including beginners, and make the community more accessible. If I were a new skater and I saw someone doing a backflip in a bowl that was a straight, cis, white lady, I'd be afraid to put skates on."

The page grew, amassing over nineteen thousand followers, and Sepi was able to use her reach to fundraise for several different organizations, including the Ryan Montgomery Foundation, which coordinates free care and access to mental health services in underserved populations; Black Girls Code; the Milwaukee Freedom Fund, which pays bail in a movement to end pretrial detention; the People's Institute for Survival and Beyond, which supports antiracist organizing and community workshops; Brave Space Alliance, the first Black-led, trans-led LGBTQ+ center located on the South Side of Chicago; the Navajo and Hopi Families COVID-19 Relief Fund; the Lebanese Red Cross; a mutual aid fund for LGBTQIA and BIPOC people affected by COVID-19; and more.

Being able to raise money for important causes was rewarding, though burnout crept in.

"I felt an intense weight on my shoulders. Because every piece of information that came out, like this person is racist or this person is homophobic, I had to have a response from the page. And it was like, am I going to say the right thing? Am I going to help people and make an impact?" she said. "A lot of people would get mad at me. I'd get angry messages from people like, 'Why haven't you responded to this? Did you know about this thing? You should say something.' I'm not going to immediately have a response. I might need to formulate my thoughts for a couple of hours. I finally posted something that said, 'I'm sorry, I'm one person and I work full time and I do this for fun in my spare time because I care. So please don't send me angry messages while I was at work and I wanted to write something thoughtful, which actually takes time.'"

There are a million wonderful things about the skating community, though it doesn't exist apart from the world. The skating community is a microcosm of the public at large; the same forces and hate that perpetuate all the nasty -isms in the larger world also manifest in the skate community. Running an Instagram account as large as BIPOC Who Skate exposed Sepi to constant news of all the bad actors in skating, and it's a lot to keep up with.

"You don't stop being racist and transphobic and homophobic just because you have skates on your feet," she said. "Those people are still awful people, and when you feign diversity, equity, and inclusion, it's dangerous because you don't actually know that you're unsafe. You can slap 'diverse, equitable, and inclusive' on anything these days and it's dangerous for people who are not cis white hetero men or women."

After seeing more specific Instagram accounts pop up for Black skaters, Indigenous skaters, Middle Eastern and North African skaters, and more, Sepi decided to stop posting to the page. It was too much pressure for one person. Instead, she turned her attention to making a difference in another way.

"I wanted to focus my time and effort less on internet things and more on helping people in a way that enriched my life," Sepi said, gesturing to a block print she carved from a chunk of rubber to raise money for the Palestinian Children's Relief Fund. The print features an outline of Palestine with hearts radiating outward from the center and a line from Emma Lazarus: "Until we are all free, we are none of us free." "Art is enriching and meditative for me," Sepi said. "I can still fundraise and help people through that."

Sepi joined forces with Olive K., a Milwaukee native who started the Queer Skate Alliance Instagram page and who previously worked for Chaya Skates and Juice Wheels, to start Radical Wheels. They wanted to design skate wheels with their art and donate a portion of the proceeds to organizations they believed in. Donating was built into their business model from the beginning.

"If our small company can do it, big skate brands could've done it from day one. But giving back wasn't important to those people," Sepi said. "It only became important when pages like Queer Skate Alliance and BIPOC Who Skate demanded it, and now other people are demanding it. It's marketing. It's just saving their asses, saving their brands."

Look no further than a couple of roller skate companies' product launches for examples. One company released a rainbow roller skate, and the community demanded they donate a portion of the proceeds to an LGBTQ+ nonprofit because by creating a rainbow skate and using language around inclusivity for the queer community, they were obviously eager to profit off the queer dollar. The LGBTQ+ community, wise to the ways of rainbow capitalism, wasn't having it. When a second roller skate company released a rainbow skate, they said up front they were donating a portion of the proceeds to avoid the same social media backlash the previous company had received.

"You find your group of friends that have the same values and want to do cool stuff. That's how Radical was born," Sepi said. "From day one, we wanted to donate part of the profits to a charity of our choosing. Every six months we'll send them a lump sum."

Having launched during the pandemic, they were preparing to send their first check at the time of my visit. They chose the Brown Boi Project, a community of masculine-of-center womyn, men, two-spirit people, transmen, and allies committed to changing the way that communities of color talk about gender. Skaters have been loving Radical Wheels both because of their mission and because the wheels are damn good. They were thoughtfully designed—the first wheel they released are 82A hardness, good for more advanced outdoor skaters; the eighties-style sunset-themed art is on the inside of the wheel so it doesn't rub off the first time you fall; and the wheel is taller than most roller skate wheels, so you get more speed and distance.

Both the BIPOC Who Skate Instagram and Radical Wheels were a response to a growing problem in the skate community.

"White influencer culture has come into roller skating, and it's even more about likes and follows and ads and making money off Instagram," she said. "As the community gets bigger, people want to be influencers, and they want to be better than everyone else when they should be valuing community over competition."

But that white influencer culture comes with the expectation of being online all the time and constantly creating content to be consumed. And some followers don't seem to understand that it takes far more time to create content than it does to consume it. Dan has noticed this too.

"I get to talk to people who are losing their sight and find my page, and helping those people out is rad," he said. "But Instagram takes a lot of work. You have to post every day, and I don't always have the time or resources to make videos every day. It's a weird world. If you don't post for a while, people will just stop following you. It's awkward."

It's a fine balance. Participating in the online community aspect of the skate world allows you to show the world the way you want to be seen. The public constantly makes assumptions about disabled people and BIPOC people, and through skating, and sharing their skating online, people from these groups can speak for themselves. It's when followers get so used to seeing people who post content on social media with the obvious intent of getting internet famous and getting free goods, and they come to expect that same type of content from the very creators who are challenging that narrative. In a situation like that, sharing your truths can begin to feel draining and even toxic.

"It's made for having fun. [Skating] wasn't created for getting likes on Instagram or getting sponsored or being cool or famous or whatever. It was made for having fun," Dan said.

When Sepi and I started to put on our skates, her bluetick hound took off with my compression socks in his mouth.

"Atlas! Come back here!" Sepi shouted.

Atlas ran circles around the garage in the softening rain, dodging Sepi at every turn, feinting left then right in a game of keep-away. When she finally lured him back into the garage, I saw that the pair of socks he grabbed were polka-dotted with rainbow hearts. Though I hadn't thought to check when I bought them, I'm pretty sure the sock company didn't donate a portion of the proceeds to an LGBTQ+ organization.

Next, Atlas stole one of Sepi's skates—"*Atlas!*"—though it was so heavy that he didn't make it far. We laughed until our stomachs hurt and ate slices of cheese, pepperoni, and mushroom pizza in between taking turns on her garage ramp.

Community isn't just online. It's not just on big ramps where impressive videos can be filmed. Community is right here, two skaters from far-flung parts of the country having made the Midwest home, skating one-on-one in a garage.

And neither of us filming a damn thing.

Cleveland, Ohio

THE KING OF CLEVELAND COMPETITION

Cleveland is old as American cities go, especially midwestern cities. It's also a city I hadn't spent much time in: I'd taken weekend trips to visit a friend there, gone to the art museum, shopped the bookstores, gone to a show in Playhouse Square, watched a baseball game, and collected land shells and sea glass—lake glass? mermaid tears?—along the beachy shore of Lake Erie. But each of these destinations had been my purpose for visiting, so I had traveled to them with a singular focus, never giving myself time to meander the city or get lost for the sake of finding my way to somewhere I wouldn't have thought to go.

I heard about the King of Cleveland rollerblade contest a few days before the event and made a last-minute decision to attend. My decision was so last-minute, in fact, that I didn't know that it would be the way I'd finally get my meandering tour of the city.

The King of Cleveland contest was in its ninth and final year. As a street contest, it made use of Cleveland's variety of unintentional skate obstacles, roving to a handful of different spots around the city. The exact locations weren't announced until the day of, so competitors had little time to train on those specific obstacles. Those who did well in the contest weren't just good on one type of obstacle but were versatile enough to nail tricks on whatever was thrown their way.

The first stop of the 2021 contest was a large planter ledge in the middle of a turnaround in a park. To get to the ledge, we walked past a makeshift memorial of two dozen veladoras, the prayer candles favored by Spanish Catholics, and the words "RIP my love <3 Long Live DJ." A bouquet of flowers was pressed into the grass nearby. The ofrenda seemed fitting with the ledge, which was painted a chipping bright yellow and shaped like a coffin with an extra corner jutting out from the side.

King of Cleveland is not a formal contest. There's no set order the competitors go in, and no names are called beforehand. The bladers take the opportunities they see, which sometimes leads to multiple skaters ending up on the same obstacle at the same time. It is, in a word, chaotic.

Other park-goers started to approach the fringes of our group to watch, and I noticed a few of them had skates on themselves. They'd ventured from deeper within the park, where there was a tennis court or basketball court with a flat surface, and had come to see the show. It's the contest's chaos that makes it so entertaining to watch. The bladers have to be intensely aware of their surroundings, not just because the obstacle itself is one they likely haven't skated before but also because they have to time their tricks so as not to collide with one another.

There is, too, the problem of cops.

"At the end of the day, it's property damage. There's no easy way to spin it," said Brandon Lorenzo Thompson, CEO of BladeCle and one of the primary organizers of King of Cleveland. "There are aspects of skating that will always be underground and that's street skating. Until we get to the point where we can build our own street-sanctioned event . . . and they try to do that now. They put a handrail and some stairs in a skate park but it's still a skate park. But I think street skating should always exist."

The underground appeal of street skating that makes it so captivating is also the very thing that makes it risky. Most people won't think twice about a handrail, a ledge, a curb, or a set of stairs until a blader shows up to skate it—then suddenly, there's outsized public rage. The cops are called. Skaters are harassed and shooed away, ticketed, or arrested.

As a veteran contest organizer, Brandon came prepared. He carried a megaphone and announced that "Baker Mayfield"—then the quarterback for the Cleveland Browns—was the code word. If Brandon shouted that, we were all supposed to scatter to the next contest location.

"You have to be smart about planning. If you're worried about a spot getting busted, make sure that the next spot isn't across the street. It's simple things like that. You have to make sure that you're putting ten minutes of distance between what you're doing to keep the fuzz off your back," Brandon explained. "And you have to consider parking. Ideally, you want a good skate spot with decent parking and low bust potential. It's a tall task."

And that's how I got my meandering tour of Cleveland, driving the ten to fifteen minutes between skate spots. The second competition site was a gnarly rail at the edge of the Detroit-Superior Bridge in the Ohio City neighborhood. The rail was thicker than typical ramp coping, though that didn't seem to worry the bladers. Neither did the fact that the rail was rusted, broken on the far end, and that it had a kink knocked into it where a car had gotten too acquainted with it. Met with another challenge, the chaos of the competition began anew.

The rail was long enough that only the most talented bladers managed to stay on until its jagged, bitter end. And it was high enough off the ground that it took a massive leap to even get enough air to lock onto it, so someone pulled a homemade quarter-pipe from their car to give the bladers more momentum. Watching the skaters pop from the top of the ramp onto the rail and ride it until they spun off was like watching someone play human pinball—the ramp as the batting arm, the rail as the wall the ball hopes to follow for its length.

As with the previous spot, people with other wheels stopped to watch. A group of skateboarders zoomed through the crosswalk to get a closer look, but they viewed from a distance as though not wanting to let the rollerbladers know that the skateboarders thought they were cool. Later, a band of cyclists stopped by, some on BMX bikes and a few on makeshift, welded-together bikes that held the riders aloft like the big-wheeled tricycles of the 1800s. They came downhill off the Detroit-Superior Bridge, hooting and popping wheelies. From an outsider's perspective, the skate scene in Cleveland appeared vibrant, varied, and visible despite the underground nature of street skating.

"The Cleveland skate scene is meh," Brandon said, surprising me. "There are so many people here who skate but only like twenty to twenty-five people who have skated in the past two to three years. It's the same six people that skate at least once a week. Or people who come to skate one time and you never hear from them again, but the whole time they're there, they're like, 'This is so fun.' I understand life happens, but it just sucks. We have a lot of really flaky rollerbladers."

Brandon started blading when he was seven and is still at it nearly thirty years later, so he holds the skate scene in Cleveland to a high standard. This is also due in part to his time in the Air Force, where he bladed at the skate park on Lackland Air Force Base in Texas, all over South Korea and Qatar while he was stationed there, and around Montgomery, Alabama, while he was stationed at Maxwell Air Force Base. He's also traveled throughout the Midwest, going to rollerblading contests for years. It's in comparing Cleveland to cities like Detroit and Chicago that made him feel like the skate scene in Cleveland is lukewarm.

"Chicago and Detroit are entirely self-sufficient. They could have their contests and not have a single person from out of town show up and it would still be a huge success. They have twenty-plus people who are putting on rollerblades and doing crazy shit every week," Brandon said. "There's not a lot of consistent rollerbladers in Cleveland, but I see skateboarders and roller skaters and we've become friends with a lot of them over the years."

As I watched the competitors shred, I wondered how many of them were from Cleveland or currently lived there. (Brandon told me later it's six or eight, which meant a dozen or so had come from out of town.) A local magazine interviewed Brandon and the other King of Cleveland organizers, Jimmy Spetz and Brent Hopkins, in 2017 and titled the article "The Last Inline." The piece made it sound like they were members of an endangered species, participants in a sport in such decline that it was carving its own tombstone. But watching the King of Cleveland contest, as well as how spectators reacted to it, it was hard for me to sense what exactly was dying.

"I've never felt like rollerblading was a dying art," Brandon said. "I just think that new people weren't really coming into the sport, and those of us who were doing it were just going to continue doing it—maybe at a lower level—forever."

But by the third contest spot—a thigh-high round bar rail that stretched the length of a long walkway—it was difficult to imagine what a lower level of rollerblading might look like. Even on a rail with no changes in elevation (as opposed to a stair rail), the bladers were doing tricks like they were performing a circus highwire act. Though, compared to past years, the 2021 King of Cleveland was fairly tame.

"We did the Browns stadium rails, which are famous here. They're famous because they're very deadly. The top of the rails is a freeway entrance, and the bottom of the rails is a freeway exit," he said. "We put cones out so we could get the inside lane on both sides. I stood at the top and Adam stood at the bottom wearing bright yellow vests so cars would slow down. The police drove through like three times and didn't say anything."

The bladers eluded the cops then, though they hadn't always. There was a reason for the "Baker Mayfield" code word.

"Another time, there was a situation where spot four was on one side of the high school and spot five was around back of the high school, and they'd randomly put up a gate around spot five, but we had a cutter. The plan was that we would go to skate spot four and somebody would go over and cut the chain on spot five real quick," Brandon began. "So we're at spot four and the police roll up. I go talk to them and they're like, 'Somebody said you were using a grinder to cut a chain,' and I said, 'They probably meant these dudes are grinding rails over here!' The cops totally didn't buy it."

Brandon continued, "One time, we got kicked out of a spot instantly and when we got to the backup spot, the rail we wanted to skate had been torn out the day before, so it was just a bunch of gravel. Then we had to think of *another* spot, so we went to a church in Ohio City and the cops pulled up on us there. After that contest, they put caps on those rails like right away." He laughed.

There's always a risk involved with street contests, though skaters getting injured worries Brandon more than the cops. Although it's not his fault, and though injury is always a possibility with an extreme sport, he takes it hard when bladers get injured at his contests—one of the reasons the contest this time around was slightly more subdued than in past years.

"I wanted to bring the danger factor down," Brandon said. "My goal was to have a weekend where people didn't get hurt."

The fourth spot in the contest was the gnarliest thus far: an eighteen-stair handrail from a sidewalk along a major street down a forty-five-degree angle into the Cleveland Cultural Gardens, a park featuring sculptures representing various countries and ethnicities that are seen in the city's population. The rail was challenging both for its length—and if you had to jump off the side, you'd be contending with bushes and trees—and for its angle, which propelled skaters down *fast*.

To successfully skate it, bladers had to jump strategically enough to get their skates locked onto the rail, and they had to stay on it while they were flung precipitously downward. An astronomical amount of precision is needed to skate this rail. For context, on the skateboarding street course for the Olympics, the longest and steepest handrail covers eleven stairs, and the grade is gentler than forty-five degrees. If rollerblading were in the Olympics, these bladers would be competing.

The spectators settled in, and you could almost hear the collective intake of breath every time a blader approached the rail. There were false starts while they got the feel of the rail and a few times where they flipped entirely over it, almost doing a gymnastics trick in an instinctual move to save themselves from crashing. None wore helmets.

It was on this obstacle that the competitors really distinguished themselves. For Ryan Parker, the rail was like a path for a spinning top. He spun to mount the rail, changed directions while flying down it, and three-sixtied in his dismount. Philip Moore executed their tricks with such calmness that they appeared no more exhausted than if they'd been walking down the street. Adam Bazydlo rendered every spectator open-mouthed when he skated across the main road at the top of the rail, waited until there was no traffic, gained speed, and got enough momentum to jump over all eighteen stairs entirely while doing a five-forty spin.

And when Brad Magnuson—who performed well throughout the contest—came off the rail so fast that he slammed into a tree hard enough to collapse half of one of his lungs, one of the *oh fuck*s from the audience was surely Brandon's. When Brad took off his shirt to inspect the damage, I noticed that his tattoo of the outline of the state of Minnesota looked as though it'd been colored in, crosshatched with scratches from the tree bark.

I recalled Tim Schmidt at Schmidty's Ramp & Camp telling me how rollerbladers prided themselves on doing the most extreme tricks they could imagine in the nineties to prove that they could go bigger and harder than skateboarders in some unspoken feud the two groups had. For those with the skills to pull it off, that propensity toward extreme tricks is alive and well in blading culture.

Rollerblading has experienced lulls just as skateboarding and roller skating have in decades past, but after what I'd seen, it was hard for me to believe that it would ever die. Rather, since I'd heard time and time again that roller skating boomed during the pandemic, I figured that rollerblading would have seen an increase too.

"People are rollerblading more, mostly recreational, but I've seen a lot of aggressive rollerbladers start coming back," Brandon said. "It's been a struggle at times to stay with it for me. I'll take a long break from it and think I don't need it, then I'll go do it and I remember why I do it. Right now, I don't have a lot of time for rollerblading because I have a sixty-five-hour-a-week job. I've only skated like five times in the past three to four months, which sucks, but I think about it every day."

I sensed he was disappointed by this, like he was worried he was turning into one of the flaky rollerbladers he mentioned, and though it may sound hypocritical on the surface, nearly every skater I talked to has expressed that at one time, they were in a situation similar to Brandon's. Rollerblading is, for the majority of its practitioners, not a profitable enterprise. Even the best bladers are more often than not forced to get day jobs or do other work to support the habit. Though the inliners at King of Cleveland would be at the level equivalent of the MLB or the NFL, there's no such professional organization to elevate the sport, no agents to bargain for higher pay, no one selling tickets for spectators to watch these competitions.

Donations are encouraged, however, to pad the winners' purses, and this is where Brandon's talents as a contest organizer really shine. It's more than picking skate spots around the city. Organizing a successful contest means raising enough money for the winners that it's worth it for people to come from out of town and out of state to compete.

"For our first contest, we only tried to raise like $1,000 or $1,500," Brandon said. "The next year was about increasing the money and getting more merchandise out. By then, we were pretty good and could get $2,000 or $2,500. Which, for a street contest, is a fairly recent thing, probably within the last three or four years. When we first started, a $1,000 first place was pretty common."

The money comes from a variety of places. The bladers pay twenty dollars each to compete, and there are sponsorship packages from businesses, T-shirt sales, and donations from individuals who want to see the contest happen. Mostly, it's a lot of Brandon sliding into people's DMs and asking if they can spare a twenty. He posts about the contests on social media and has gotten savvy to the ways of marketing. For what to an outsider might look like a bunch of delinquent street rats destroying property for entertainment, Brandon's work has given a new level of legitimacy to street contests.

The events aren't just important for the bladers who feel more at home in the concrete jungles of the urban landscape than the undulating curves of the skate park. They also help fight the negative stigma that follows rollerbladers in the larger skating world.

"There's a huge stigma against rollerbladers from people who have never seen the contests and the tricks. They just see people blading on the sidewalk around the park and are like, 'That shit's gay,' but anybody who sees a rollerblading contest is impressed," Brandon said.

In his twenty-seven years of rollerblading, Brandon has been harassed, ridiculed, and discriminated against dozens of times—both for being Black and for his choice of wheels. It even happened at a previous King of Cleveland event.

"We were going to have the contest at Fun Wall [a publicly accessible outdoor DIY that has since been demolished], and the skateboarders there were pricks. They'd say, 'We built all this stuff and if you want to donate money you can,' but donate money turned into, 'You have to pay to skate here.' I ignored them, but some people I was with paid them. It wasn't even the dude who built it; it was that dude's friend's friend's friend. So all those dudes were grifting people so they could buy heroin to shoot up," Brandon said, scoffing at the memory. Had the bladers been a group of skateboarders, they likely wouldn't have been hassled.

"It's been a constant problem my whole life," Brandon added. "I've been skating for a very long time, and the bullshit and the bullying has been a problem forever. I stopped caring ten to fifteen years ago. I pushed through it, like, I'm here doing my thing, so fuck off."

Things are getting better. As the long moral arc of the universe bends toward justice and the skating world evolves with time, things like racism, sexism, homophobia, and fighting over the vessel with which one chooses to skate feel like attitudes of the old guard.

"It's really stopped being a problem—like fully, no negativity involved—in the past three years. Three years ago was the first time I heard people be like, 'Oh, you rollerblade?' in a positive way. The tone changed," he said.

That's due in part to the new generation of rollerbladers, some of whom put on inlines for the first time during the pandemic.

"Generation Z has surprised me. They've broken a barrier that we were never able to break, which is inclusivity. Rollerblading has always been used as a derogatory term, that it's for 'fags' and 'gay people do it,' and Gen Z don't play that shit," Brandon explained. "That has really changed the landscape because a lot of people in our generation who wouldn't have been able to look at rollerblading because of the negative stigma that's attached to it are now able to consider it because that negative stigmatization is being pushed back on by Generation Z. They're enjoying what they're doing and are not worried about what anybody else thinks about what they do or look like."

Perhaps it's not rollerblading that's dying but rollerblading as we've historically known it. Inline skating, with its waxing and waning popularity over the decades, will live on, but with any luck, the bigoted attitudes that have accompanied it will become relics of the past.

"I've always had the philosophy that if you're not changing, you're not growing," said Brandon. "This is another aspect of that change."

He's not just talking about the culture around rollerblading becoming more accepting. The other "this" he's referring to is that after the 2021 event, the contest will be going through an evolution. Instead of having the contest in Cleveland every year, it'll move to different cities around

Ohio. Columbus, Toledo, and Cincinnati are all on the immediate list, and the contest's name will change to King of Ohio. It'll give the bladers in each city time to plan an excellent contest while also not burning out all the spots in Cleveland. They already have nonbinary skaters who have competed and won the King of Cleveland title, so perhaps they'll change the name too, especially if women choose to compete.

"I see a lot of contests that say, well, we did good last year, so let's rinse and repeat. That's wack. If you're not evolving with the culture then what are you doing? You have to always be upping it," Brandon said. "So this is the next big, dramatic change. And if it's a complete failure, we'll do something else."

Although Brandon has devoted so much time to organizing contests, he's adamant that rollerblading doesn't have to be competitive, and at the end of the day, he just wants people to enjoy having blades on their feet.

"People are going to put on skates and they're going to see somebody do a grind and be like, 'I want to do that!' And others are going to see somebody do a grind and say, 'I'm *never* gonna do that.' It doesn't matter how good you are. If you just put skates on, you'll get enjoyment out of it and where you want to take it from there is up to you," he said.

"I'm going to do it for as long as I can, even if it's not aggressive," he told me. "I'm going to do it forever."

Rutland, Ohio

SKATOPIA

Twenty-five miles from the nearest interstate and seven miles from the nearest highway, Skatopia is where those of us from Appalachia might call "yonder." Rutland is closer to West Virginia than any of Ohio's major cities. The only thing preventing me from saying it is a holler is that a holler is a low place between two hills, and Skatopia is atop a hill—and a steep one at that.

My twenty-year-old Camry was no match for the gravel drive. We slowly passed the signs reading "Skatopia: Enter At Your Own Risk!" and "No Law Enforcement Beyond This Point," as well as the folk-art decor: a skateboard crashed through a television screen, plastic skeletons from Halloweens of yore left hanging year-round in the trees, and, under a carport, a giant skateboard larger than my vehicle. At about that point, my wheels started to spin and my car rolled backward. I burned rubber trying to get traction but ultimately left the Camry parked where it sat, which happened to be right next to the skateboard museum.

At least, I reasoned, being so close to the collection of hundreds of vintage skateboards meant my car wasn't likely to be burned.

"This place has 'yeehaw, fuck the law' vibes," I said to my husband, Jon.

"I don't think they even acknowledge the law enough to fuck it," he replied.

Out of all my skate travels, Skatopia was the only place my husband insisted on accompanying me to. I couldn't blame him. When I told other skaters I was visiting the anarchist skate commune, home of the CIA—or Citizens Instituting Anarchy—they all said, "Be careful! I heard that place is dangerous," and, "How will you get home if they burn your car?" After watching the 2010 documentary *Skatopia: 88 Acres of Anarchy* and looking up the criminal record of its founder, Brewce Martin (Jon is a journalist and former crime reporter, after all), my partner decided to come with me even though he doesn't skate.

It was ninety-six degrees on the day we visited, and the heat index was into the triple digits. I thought I'd faint just walking farther up the drive to get to the skate park buildings. There were several: the pipe, which was nearly a full pipe ramp with only the very top open; the Epcot Bean Bowl, which is affectionately called the Punisher for its thirteen-foot vertical drop; the Church Bowl, which is inside a Quonset hut with an upside-down cross at the apex, marking it as a church of skatan; and the Lula Bowl, a gigantic concrete bowl with a school bus built into one side for especially creative tricks.

As we trekked up the hill on foot, a pack of semi-feral dogs greeted us; they seemed to pour from spots of shade underneath an old pickup truck, under the edges of the full pipe, and from the wooden deck surrounding the Punisher. They howled a warning, stopping us, as a man appeared on the deck looking down.

He looked like a shirtless Gandalf with half the hair, complete with you-shall-not-pass energy. He had arresting arctic blue eyes and the many-lined, weathered face of a wizard, or someone who's spent years surviving on the streets using his wits.

"Hi," I called up to him. "Are you Brewce?"

"No, I'm Tim. Tim Tice. Tice like mice like rice," he replied, as though he'd said it a thousand times.

Although I didn't know it then, he was just the man I was looking for.

Much has been written (and filmed) about Skatopia's founder, Brewce Martin. He's been called a cult leader, an abuser, a god, and Sk8 Pope. A professional skateboarder in the nineties, Martin, who was originally from West Virginia, bought the land he'd turn into Skatopia in Meigs County, Ohio, after being evicted, fined, or otherwise discouraged from building skate ramps and throwing parties at other places he'd lived. As an anarchist, he doesn't believe that government is necessary for organizing society, and he especially doesn't believe the government has a right to tell you what you can and cannot do on your own land. Not content with the small-scale DIYs secreted away in cities and country towns the nation over, he wanted something bigger, grander, and more permanent—something to call his own. Brewce went about as far as one can go in securing money and a room of one's own to build Skatopia.

Though he owns the land, every problem a DIY spot might have is magnified at Skatopia. It's hard to keep track of exactly how much Brewce has spent on the skate park because he's built it slowly over the course of nearly three decades and has used recycled materials, volunteer labor, monetary donations from visitors, and cash collected in shakedowns after wild Bowl Bash parties. However, it's not a stretch to say that it's a million-dollar skate park. For the average person or municipality to build a similar facility, a million dollars would be a conservative estimate. Skatopia has been plagued by financial troubles for years, including an attempted foreclosure on the property in the mid-2000s. On top of that, it struggles with people who show up on the property because they hear it's an anarchist utopia and hope to live there without having to work or financially contribute. But someone has to buy the beer. Someone has to build and maintain the ramps. Someone has to ensure the bills get paid, that concrete is poured, and that the acres and acres and acres of grass get mowed.

This is not to say that Brewce hasn't courted trouble. He's been incarcerated multiple times and has a rap sheet a mile long. The *Meigs*

Independent Press reported on one of the more recent times he ran afoul of the law: he'd beaten up the boyfriend of a woman he fancied. When that wasn't enough to send the fellow heading for the hills, Brewce saw him filling up at a gas station and shouted, "I'm going to fucking kill you!" before attempting to run him over. The man made it out alive, skirting death and Brewce's rage once again. A Meigs County jury convicted him of misdemeanor assault. There is, too, a GoFundMe alleging Brewce abused his former girlfriend, Halo, with whom he has a daughter, and that the daughter, now a teenager, is so traumatized by him that she doesn't want a relationship. He's confessed in many interviews that he's impulsive and has anger issues. It's been said that his impulsivity has only gotten worse following a head injury about a decade ago. A tire exploded in his face, and part of his skull had to be removed to relieve the pressure on his brain. He still has the chunk of skull.

This is to say that what newspaper articles revealed about Brewce's personality, combined with the car burnings, firework mortars, violent mosh pits, guns, and hard drugs I saw in the documentary, he scared the ever-loving shit out of me.

When I asked Tim if Brewce was around, he replied that Brewce was "out of town on business," and I wondered if I should take that to mean that he was in prison. I tried to imagine better options: perhaps he was visiting a skate friend? I'll admit to a sort of willful denial. In order to visit Skatopia and minimize the likelihood of me having a panic attack even after taking a double dose of my anxiety medication, I had to convince myself, at least for the day, that Brewce wasn't as bad as his reputation foretold. I reminded myself that he raised his son, Brandon, as a single father (intentionally not stopping to consider what kind of father he might have been) and that for a number of lost and wayward souls, he's been a source of inspiration. Over the years, Skatopia has been a temporary haven, a sort of enabling halfway house, for people who don't have a home to return to and no one to miss them. I had to remind myself that professional skateboarders from Tony Hawk (who included Skatopia in his legendary video game series *Tony Hawk Pro Skater*) to Bam Margera, and countless others from all over the world, have made the pilgrimage to Skatopia and—as far as I know—made it out alive.

I later found out, through some research, that Brewce very likely was incarcerated when I was there. He was arrested in early 2021 by the Bureau of Alcohol, Tobacco, Firearms, and Explosives on a charge of knowingly possessing a firearm after having been convicted of a misdemeanor crime of domestic violence. A past domestic violence conviction made it illegal for him to own a gun, much less the several that were found on his property, including an automatic machine gun. From what I could tell, the pandemic—or perhaps a backlog in the federal court—bought him some time as a free man. At the time of my visit, the last update on the docket said Brewce was to be detained at least until his pretrial conference, which was scheduled for August 9. We unknowingly had come to visit Skatopia that very week. (Brewce was released from prison on November 9, 2022.)

I'm less concerned with attempting to make sense of Brewce, and I have no desire to defend a man simply because he built a legendary skate park. I'm more concerned for Skatopia's future. Brewce is in his late fifties and suffering from the aftereffects of that head injury, and his son Brandon, whose name is on the deed to the property, is also having some health issues that prevent him from being fully present at Skatopia. The pandemic has prevented them from hosting big parties like they have in the past, which means they have less money coming in for maintenance. It's also quite possible the place's hardcore party reputation frightens off a contingent of skaters who might otherwise be interested in making the expedition to skate there.

For skaters, especially skateboarders, Skatopia is the equivalent of a UNESCO World Heritage Site. It's the kind of place you hear about your entire life and have on your bucket list to visit. It's the kind of place you want to see live on, even if that means it outlives its founder.

After forty-five minutes of trying to skate the pipe and the Church Bowl and nearly passing out from the heat, I headed back to find Tim.

The dogs started up again with my approach, but he was already waiting for me.

"I meet and greet everybody that comes up here. There's very few people that come up that driveway without me seeing them," he said. "I got the dogs. There's a difference in the bark when you first got here and when you came down the hill just now."

Tim led me and Jon through the wooden deck between the full pipe and the Punisher Bowl to his room. He's got a bedroom and a kitchen area built into the structure of the ramp, so he can essentially roll out of bed and be ten feet away from being able to drop in on what many would consider two of the gnarliest ramps in the country.

Tim was born in the West Virginia panhandle, and one fateful day in 1964, he was staying home from school because he was sick and turned on the TV. He didn't know it then, but what he saw would change his life.

"This girl skateboarder, Patti McGee, came on live TV. She was barefooted and doing tic-tacs and three-sixties and I was like, 'Wow! She's gorgeous!'" Tim said. "I was five or six years old at the time and never forgot it."

Patti McGee was a champion skateboarder and surfer in 1964 and 1965. What Tim saw on TV was her setting the world record for the fastest girl on a skateboard—at forty-seven miles per hour—at Dick Clark's World Teen Fair at the Orange County Fairgrounds in California. (The record has since been broken.)

Tim comes from an athletic family. They spent a lot of time skiing and ice skating, and his first three bikes kept getting bent because, inspired by Evel Knievel, he kept jumping ramps. But it was skateboarding that took hold, especially after he and his family took a 1970 trip to Huntington Beach, California, to visit relatives.

"I saw the pier, and the skaters were hitting this bank. A kid lost his skateboard, and I put my foot on it to stop it from getting too far away and he says, 'Go ahead!' So I said, 'Okay!'" Tim said. "I put my hands down to slide around like I would when I'd ice skate, and people were clapping. It was like, huh? What'd I do?"

He didn't care much for tricks, but he was having fun, and that's what mattered most to him. Still does. When he returned from that summer in California, his junior high school picture told the story of who he aspired to be as an adult.

"I had my hair parted in the center and a sunburn from California. Being out there totally changed my persona," he said. "I wanted to be like them out there. I wanted to do the surf and skate thing."

Tim became a nomadic hippie adventurer, hitchhiking from Michigan to Southern California, New Orleans, Florida, and back to Michigan. He'd take his harmonica and play on the street for money. It was on one of his stops in Florida, at Daytona Beach, that Tim met Brewce Martin for the first time.

"I met a pipe fitter on a job site who was wearing a Thrasher hat, and I was like, 'Hey, you skate?' He says, 'Yeah, and I got this guy you're going to want to meet. We'll go skate at this new skate park,'" Tim said. "So I meet this guy who was in Daytona for college, and he's like the He-Man. Short guy but real powerful and with this charisma like a cult leader. People would follow him around because he had such great energy."

Some time later, Tim moved in with Brewce, who had recently gotten custody of his five-year-old son.

"I gravitate towards men who take care of their families, no child support or nothing. I'd babysit him so Brewce could go do things," he said.

Eventually, Brewce moved back to West Virginia, where he's originally from, and rented a house where he built a ramp.

"We went up there, and it was this big festival, like Burning Man, but everybody was skating. There was a fog machine and bands playing until like four in the morning. Then you'd sleep it off in a tent and go home. There was partying going on, but I'd drink coffee at night while they're hitting nitrous and not skating. I decided to stay away from drinking and drugs to skate," Tim said. "They [the landlord] kicked him out after a year or two."

It was the eviction that inspired Brewce to search out property of his own and planted the seed for what would eventually become Skatopia. For him, the concept of freedom became irrevocably tied to owning land.

In the following years, Tim was working for another pro skateboarder, Bob Burnquist, in Vista, California. Bob's home includes a world-renowned private skate park called Dreamland, which features, among other obstacles, a vert bowl and a megaramp. Tim, being both a skater and all-around talented craftsman and handyman, helped build Dreamland. Meanwhile, Skatopia was still being added onto, so Brewce reached out to his old friend and asked Tim to be a part of it.

"I was always down for Brewce's energy and magnanimous personality, so I said okay, I'll go help him out, see how his injury is doing," Tim said, speaking of Brewce's 2009 accident incident where a tire exploded in Brewce's face and left him in critical condition for weeks and with a permanent plate in his skull. "The first month I got here, I fixed all the showers and all the toilets. Then I started on remodeling all the kitchens and making this place livable. I planted a hundred fruit trees. To me it was a labor of love. I'd work in the mornings, go help him out, then come back and skate."

Tim lives at Skatopia and receives room and board in exchange for his labor. Being an anarchist, he doesn't believe in government and chooses to only take labor that wouldn't force him to pay taxes, which he hasn't done in three decades. He and Brewce have a symbiotic relationship. Tim sees this exchange as his way of contributing time, labor, and spiritual currency to keep this dream alive.

Listening to Tim tell the story of how he came to live at Skatopia is like talking to a man who's lived a thousand lives. He's been coast to coast and seen so much in between. He's relied on the kindness of strangers and been a kind stranger to others. He's the kind of person you think exists only in a movie, like the holistic surf-and-skate version of the cowboy in *The Big Lebowski*. He waxes poetic about skateboarding while also weaving in rants about how Columbus didn't discover a damn thing, how white supremacists are stupid, why processed food will kill you, and his theories on how to defeat the Illuminati. When he talks about Skatopia, he makes it sound like an ashram.

Tim is also sixty-two years old. Though he's far spryer than most people his age, a benefit of his constant movement—whether it's skateboarding or finding work to do on the property—Tim won't be able to keep the Skatopia dream alive forever.

"What's going to happen in the future, we don't know. It's time now to band together and keep this place open," he implored. "We need some kind of committee or a group of people who come here and collect all the donations and make it work. Brewce doesn't think he needs any help, but it's like, no, you need help. I'd like to at least see him keep his head out of the garbage, separating cans," Tim added, referring to a recycling facility a few towns over that will accept aluminum cans and pay a few cents apiece.

Tim has been helpful in keeping people from taking advantage of Brewce. All some people see is a former pro skateboarder who's been on TV, and they think the coffers are bottomless, so they want to skim some off the top.

"When I first came here, there was a guy selling fireworks and pocketing the money, and I said, 'Oh no, you're not going to do that on my watch.' So I said, 'Brewce, this guy just took a bunch of your money.' And Brewce goes, 'Is that true?' And the guy goes, 'Well, I was gonna give you your cut,'" Tim huffed. "Brewce says, 'Get the hell off my farm.' He was selling fireworks out of the place where we were selling food."

Skatopia needs money to stay afloat, and people who are willing to donate their time and labor to do maintenance and improvements, but they also need people to enjoy the skate park without destroying it.

"You got guys who come here and party and hang out all weekend, then they go home. But when you burn a car, I'm the one who has to scrap that thing and get rid of it. It'd be nice if you burnt a car if you stuck around long enough to clean it up. You know, we don't have big money for a pickup crew," Tim said. "It's this whole thing with skate and destroy. They go and they tag spots and break bottles and leave shit around. It's unfair for the people who have to go around and pick that shit up."

Tim scoffed, "We want to make it more inviting for everybody to come here. Nobody wants to go to a place where it's all trashed. I saw a video of this place before I came here, and it was clothes everywhere, boxes empty, trash all over the place, which is typical of Skatopia. Most people don't care about pulling the last beer out of the carton and not throwing the box away. They'll make you think there's still another beer in there."

To put it bluntly, anarchy is hard work. And often, when it comes down to somebody having to pour the concrete, somebody having to buy the beer, somebody having to make sure the grass gets mowed and the bills get paid—those somebodies are Brewce and Tim.

"I'd like to see people take care of this place. Your mom don't live here, so pick up after yourself. I say, 'You can't leave your shit laying out like that.' We need to teach these young kids who are inspired by this place but haven't really figured it out yet that if you worked as hard as Brewce did, any one of us could have something like this."

Anyone who's seen Skatopia and its sprawling skate spots built into the foothills of the Appalachians would surely agree that Brewce does work hard, at least in his singular interest of skateboarding.

"Every day he's waking people up at 6:00 or 7:00 a.m., putting them to work. He's always doing something," Tim said with admiration in his voice. "As John Wayne said, 'Put the bacon on a biscuit, we're burning daylight.'"

The challenges are many, the resources are few, and the future of Skatopia is uncertain.

"I really don't know what the future of this place is," Tim sighed. "This could be a sanctuary. That's the vision. I love this place because it's my Disney World. I'm a puppeteer, I set up the bands, put on the lights and smoke machine, run down, and sell beer. I love it."

Ideally, they want to make Skatopia into a self-sustaining farm: growing food, using solar power to get off the electric grid, collecting rainwater, saving seeds, and propagating fruit trees. They'd love to build a megaramp to attract BMXers and other kinds of skaters.

"If it's just skateboarding, then people are intimidated. You got people who want to come here, but they rollerblade or they scooter and it's like, so what? Go ahead and try!" Tim said. "We don't put anybody down. I learn from watching other people and living vicariously through them—that's spiritual. I have a lot better faith in humanity."

When I told him I roller skate on ramps, Tim said Brewce used to do the same and still has his old quads in the skateboard museum on the property. Brewce has collected hundreds of skateboards from the early 1960s to the mid-2000s. Though Skatopia was founded by a skateboarder and skateboarders make up the majority of its visitors, it's open to all wheels. That ethos extends into the place's core belief system.

"That's why we moved here, so we can say and do whatever we want. Don't tread on me. Come and take it. You're not taking my freedom. I don't want to live in an area where they say you can't do this, can't do that. Out here, people just want to be themselves," Tim said, before discussing how people can't think for themselves because they've been indoctrinated into this country's political system and the military-industrial complex.

Freedom is easy to understand in theory, though difficult in practice, especially when it's combined with anarchy. Brewce purchased land and built Skatopia as a place where freedom could thrive—to be yourself, to do whatever you want, to slough off the bounds of society and tradition like dead skin. But so often, someone's freedom comes at the expense of someone else's servitude. If skaters are free to burn their cars and leave the smoked-out husks, free to leave their trash where they drop it, Brewce and Tim have to clean up after them. But if they impose rules about littering—and they have in recent years—then there's technically a limit on others' freedom. And rules are antithetical to anarchy since anarchism is insubordination to authority. It seems that as Brewce and Tim have gotten older and are beginning to realize their own physical and energetic limitations, they've come to realize that Skatopia is, in fact, not the utopia its name implies.

Here, too, my husband came in handy. Jon studied political theory in college and spent years reporting on state government. He said there's a difference between the philosophy of anarchism—a stateless society—and a rebellion against an existing government and social structure that sometimes gets branded as anarchist but is not without its own rules and governance. Skatopia seemed less like anarchy and more like a chaotic, benevolent dictatorship or monarchy; otherwise, skaters would show up on the property and start pouring their own concrete bowls with no regard for what Brewce wanted.

In times past, visitors to Skatopia were asked to put in an hour or two of work around the property in order to skate, though they've been lax on that request for people coming in from out of town who only want to skate for a few hours.

"If you want to kick in, do insulation work or whatever, cool. We've got tools. But they shouldn't be expected to. You need people to give of themselves freely. You get more out of people if they're able to create and have fun," Tim said.

But there's always the chance that people won't lend a hand like you hope they will. Tim showed us a partially built mini-bowl behind the full pipe that he said he'd been trying to finish building for months; he needs more hands than have been offered.

Brewce and Tim aren't telling visitors a specific way they have to live and contribute. They just let people know what they need and what's encouraged, but nobody is made to do any one thing. In that way, Jon assessed, Brewce and Tim are more party hosts than utopians.

I think of the utopian societies that have been attempted throughout Ohio: the Oberlin Colony, Clermont Phalanx, Prairie Home Community, Fruit Hills, and Free Lovers, all founded on either socialist ideals, like communally owning property, or religious principles. They all sought to prove that their chosen system would work on a larger social scale. And they all failed. While I'm not naive or idealistic enough to think that Skatopia could truly live up to its name and do what no other attempted utopia has done before—actually succeed—I want to see it survive. I want to see it thrive beyond Brewce's charisma and in spite of his self-sabotage. I want to see Skatopia live on when Tim is no longer able to be its caretaker.

"I'm sixty-two, so who knows. Will I see seventy-two? I hope I'm still skating," Tim said. "It's not like I want to be the last old guy standing, it's that I know this is the path."

I arrived at Skatopia expecting the worst, but what I found is that its reputation is misleading. Outside of its scheduled parties, it's fairly calm. It feels normal, even. As afraid as I was to even go there, I wasn't expecting to feel so much affection for the place. When it was time to hit the road, I was sad to leave, and I missed being there before I'd even left. I had the sinking sense that there was an expiration date on Skatopia as we know it—that without something giving, it might not last.

TUTTLE SKATE PARK

There's a brand-new skate park in Columbus, Ohio. Although the construction was delayed for a year due to the pandemic, Tuttle Skate Park unofficially opened in spring 2021. I say "unofficially" because there was never a formal announcement or grand opening celebration—skaters regularly checked the progress of the concrete pours and rail installations and one day decided what was there was good enough. The place has been crawling with skaters ever since.

On a particularly crowded day about two weeks after its unofficial opening, the park played host to more than fifty skaters in its twelve thousand square feet of concrete. This is to say, it's not a quiet place—which is what made the whispers even stranger.

"Holy shit, look at that!"

"Dude, what the fuck?"

"No way, that's so cool!"

"Did you see that?!"

The whisper-yells made their way from one end of the skate park to the other. Among them was a word my brain couldn't process in the context of the location: "Unicycle."

Sure enough, a guy had brought his unicycle to the skate park, and having never seen anything like it, people stopped mid-skate to see what he'd do. The fellow—slender with dark coiffed hair and a day's worth of stubble—mounted the unicycle with practiced ease. He began pedaling immediately to keep his balance because there's no standing still on a unicycle. I couldn't help thinking he must have the strongest core in three counties, especially when he rolled his way down a set of stairs before turning around, gaining momentum by rolling down a mini-ramp, and then jumped into a grind on a flat bar using the pedal.

It would have been just a little too uncool to clap or cheer, but the admiring *daaaaaayum*s could be heard throughout the park. No matter what this guy did, it would be infinitely more impressive than the same trick done on anything with two, four, or eight wheels. We were enraptured. This man was doing something we didn't know was possible. He was doing the equivalent of wrestling a bear on Mars or eating a bowl of shrimp sprinkled with Skittles; until that moment, none of us could have conceived of the two going together.

The novelty of the sight is indicated in the responses Jake Bavarsky hears when people see him unicycling.

"They ask, 'Do you juggle?' or 'Where's your other wheel?'" Jake laughed. "Sometimes it's, 'Do a kickflip!' or 'Do a wheelie!' Coming back from a concert last night, someone was like, 'Oh shit, a unicycle!' and I was like, 'Oh shit, a pedestrian! Two legs, that's crazy!'"

And when people ask Jake where he got his unicycle?

"The bike store." He deadpanned and paused for dramatic effect. "It was half off!"

There's a reason you don't see many unicycles at skate parks—they're not conducive to the environment. The mechanics of unicycles don't lend themselves well to ramps because, with most unicycles, as with a fixed-gear bike, you must keep pedaling to move. You can roll down a half- or quarter-pipe, but getting back up the other side is a different story. To unicycle at a skate park is to tire out quickly.

Yet despite its challenges, Jake, whom I would later meet at a coffee shop and witness rolling through the University District on his commuter unicycle on his way there, had found a way to push the boundaries of the sport he loved. And he's not the only one. Jake was encouraged to try unicycling at skate parks after meeting Ohio State University student Nick Braun.

"I learned to unicycle like eleven years ago at my elementary school, then I stopped for about five years and picked it up again. When I picked it up again is when I started doing tricks. I watched some YouTube videos and got really into it," Nick said.

Before long, he was exploring the various sub-niches of this already niche sport.

"You have your mountain unicycling, your track races, choreographed and freestyle performances, and urban disciplines, which is the stuff you'd imagine at a skate park. There's street unicycling, which is using the elements of a skate park like stairs, ledges, and rails, then there's flatland, which is tricks on flat ground. Lastly, there's trials, which is getting over obstacles and going through a specific line without falling off," Nick said, trailing off before suddenly remembering more. "There are also some urban competitions that don't fit into the others, like the long jump and the high jump. Then there are speed trials, which is a race on a set trials course."

Even among the sport's most avid practitioners, unicycling at skate parks is fairly rare, though.

"We're really spread out. There are people in the Midwest, but sometimes it's just one person for each of these points on this Skrrrt map," Nick said, showing me a map on his phone. Skrrrt.io is a social media app specifically for unicyclists, designed to encourage meetups and knowledge sharing. Skrrrt's map shows users where the active unicyclists are throughout the world.

Skrrrt isn't the only way for unicyclists to connect. Nick runs a Discord server with more than six hundred unicyclists around the world. That's how he met Jake, and it was pure luck they both were in Columbus.

While Nick was in the city to go to OSU, Jake came to the city for work. He's a recent graduate of the University of Connecticut, which is where he learned to unicycle.

"I came to college and joined the marching band. I'd always been in the marching band in high school, but I wanted to pick an instrument that requires no musical knowledge and no musical ability, so I picked the cymbals," Jake began. "The drumline had an indoor routine they'd do for the basketball games at UConn where they would have two cymbal players on unicycles and they'd do cymbal high fives during the routine. I thought it was the dopest thing ever."

Though he'd long held out against buying anything from Amazon, Jake couldn't resist the call of a sixty-dollar unicycle, so he made his first purchase from the retail giant.

"It was a twenty-four-inch wheel, a good standard riding unicycle. For two weeks, from 10:00 p.m. to 1:00 a.m. I'd go to the parking lot and try to ride it. After two weeks, I could get on it while holding the wall for dear life and ride around. Then I bought a better unicycle and started riding it to class," Jake said. "I was so excited to start doing the cymbal high fives with the drumline, then they said we're not doing that routine anymore. So I was like, 'Now what?! I have this useless skill for nothing.'"

Jake's unicycling wasn't entirely useless, however. He kept riding to class and eventually started a unicycling club on campus. He and Nick have that in common.

"I knew I wanted to start a club here before I came to college," Nick said. He'd tried to start a unicycle club in high school, but he didn't have support from the administration, and there were always basketball practices in the gym where Nick had hoped to meet.

"It was my second semester of freshman year when I started the club with just a few friends. I didn't have any extra unicycles to teach people with, so it was people who knew how to unicycle and had their own and were willing to share," Nick said. "We'd meet every week on Sunday, and for two hours, we'd unicycle around. I'd teach people some new things. We rode around campus, just hanging out.

"Then the next semester, I was able to get like twenty unicycles from my old elementary school where I learned. The principal gave them to me for free, so I was able to use those for the club. I started advertising a bunch and got a lot of new people to join. Every week, we meet and I teach people how to unicycle," Nick said.

As with most forms of wheely sports, it's the community that keeps people coming back.

"I thought, 'I have this useless skill, so I want to find a community,'" Jake said.

He said "useless skill" not as a pejorative, but in a rather loving way. Jake's whole demeanor brightened when he talked about unicycling, and you got the sense he'd rather be unicycling than just about anything else. I read the "useless" in "useless skill" as being a hobby that's aggressively unmarketable and unmonetizable. When one is as dedicated to a hobby that is unlikely to even have the potential of earning money, it's a slap in the face to capitalism and the kinds of "useful" skills society encourages us to collect. Jake probably can't put unicycling in the skills section of his résumé unless he's auditioning for the circus, but what he gains from it is a human need as deeply entrenched and as necessary as money: belonging. The core of every strong community is a sense of belonging over a common bond, and unicycling (and skating in general) are no different.

Jake and Nick met even more unicyclists at the 2021 North American Unicycling Competition and Convention (NAUCC), which was held in Madison, Wisconsin. Together, they competed in nearly every event, including a five-mile mountain unicycling race, several road races, a 10k, and a criterium. However, even with a mass gathering of unicyclists, unicycling at skate parks isn't one of the main events.

"Unicycles at skate parks are a small subgroup of the people at the NAUCC, the smallest amount out of any of the disciplines they have because there are things that other people do that are more accessible. Like with the road races, you don't have to have any extra skills, you just have to know how to ride," Nick explained. "But it's growing, and I'm trying really hard to help it grow."

Jake also thinks there are a number of unicycling skate park-goers who just don't go to the annual competition.

"NAUCC is an event through the Unicycling Society of America, so you have to be a USA member to attend. A lot of urban riders are grassroots, like, 'I get together with my homies and we go to the skate park, but I don't care about going to a convention,'" Jake said. "So there's been a big push for us to try to get them to buy into the USA and come to the conventions, not just to come to have a place to go and have a community but to *enhance* and diversify the community."

One thing is for certain: the Unicycling Society of America has buy-in and participation from the Midwest. Out of the forty-nine annual competitions that have been held since 1972, thirty-six have taken place in the Midwest. From Michigan to South Dakota and from Ohio to Iowa, the Midwest has been well represented in terms of where unicyclists across the country choose to gather. It makes sense, then, that midwestern unicyclists would be the ones to iterate and elevate the sport.

Because skateboarding was the first of the wheely sports to be practiced in pools and, later, designated skate parks, skateboarders crafted the lexicon for tricks, and other types of skaters considered how they could apply the existing skateboarder tricks to their wheels of choice. For unicyclers, that meant figuring out how to jump onto obstacles to grind rails and ledges using the pedal and crank of the unicycle, as well as coasting, which is the skateboarding equivalent of a manual. A manual, or "mani," on a skateboard means riding while balancing only on the front or back wheels, not both. In unicycling, it's taking both feet off the pedals and continuing to roll while using one foot as a counterweight to stay balanced. Crank flips, which involve jumping and kicking the unicycle's cranks so that the wheels do a revolution or two, is the equivalent of a kickflip. Unispins, which involve jumping off the unicycle, spinning it underneath you, and landing on it again, is the equivalent of a tre flip. All these tricks can be done on the street obstacles at a skate park.

"We can't really do things on half-pipes. . . . You can only go as fast as you can physically pedal with your feet, which makes it really hard to get speed inside of a bowl. You can drop in, but once you drop in, you're done," Nick said.

While obviously not a one-to-one comparison, the likening between unicycling as an extreme sport and aggressive skateboarding isn't lost on some of skateboarding's earliest innovators. Dan Heaton, essentially the Tony Hawk of unicycling, interviewed professional skateboarder Stacy Peralta for Heaton's documentary film *Revolution One: A Story of Off-Road Unicycling*. Peralta, of Z-Boys and *Lords of Dogtown* fame, and his peers were among the first to skateboard in empty pools, inventing tricks along the way, and they are largely the reason we have skate parks today.

Peralta had this to say in *Revolution One*: "I rode a unicycle as a kid but never in my wildest imagination did I think that you guys could do what you do. . . . What's cool is you're doing on a unicycle exactly what we were doing on a skateboard thirty years ago. You're inventing a sport."

After seeing them ride, I can't help but feel Jake and Nick are among those inventing—and reinventing—the sport, one in which the lucky few of us skaters who happen to be at the skate park at the same time get to witness. People are coming up with new ways to enjoy skate parks and engage with skate culture every day, and they're doing it where you least expect it, including at a community skate park in Columbus, Ohio. We don't know what the future of skating will look like, but we know that its many forms, unicycling included, will continue to exist.

"This is just the beginning," Nick said. "Watch out for us in the next ten years. I think unicycling is going to keep growing and growing."

FAIRWOOD SKATE PARK

I t didn't take long for the video to go viral. A man rollerblading down the interstate, naked except for a giant panda head, is the stuff of internet prankster clickbait. In a matter of hours, the "story," if the thirty-second video could be called that, was picked up by local and national news outlets.

"Do you know who this is?" a reporter friend at the local public radio station texted me.

"Yep," I responded. "That's the guy who kicked in my cabin door while I was changing at skate camp. He was wearing a full panda suit and skated in with his camera rolling. *While* I was changing clothes," I emphasized.

"Yikes," my friend responded.

"It was pretty creepy," I said.

It happened so fast. A year before, I'd gone to Woodward East— one of the best skate training facilities in the country—in Woodward, Pennsylvania, for the second time. I met up with a handful of women I'd met at skate camp two weeks previously, and when we heard there was going to be another adults-only weekend, we all signed up.

We arrived Friday afternoon, snagged our spots in a cabin together, and skated well into the night. After breakfast Saturday morning, Mary and I went back to our cabin to change into our skate clothes. We were the only ones in our cabin, and we chatted freely as we changed. Everyone else was still at breakfast, and we didn't lock the door because we didn't want to keep one of the other sixteen or so skaters bunking in the cabin locked out. I also didn't care if Mary saw my boobs while I changed—she's a woman I trust.

Suddenly, our cabin door flew open so quickly that the doorknob slammed into the wall, and for a moment, all we saw was a rollerblade with a leg attached to it. I vaguely registered that someone had kicked in our door when a man skated in and made a loop through the cabin, yelling, "Wake up! We're going rollerblading today!"

The rollerblading man was carrying a selfie stick with a phone attached, and he was speaking to it. The camera was rolling—a live stream.

Just as quickly as he had entered, he disappeared with the cabin door slamming behind him. I stood there slack-jawed, trying to make sense of the previous thirty seconds.

"Jesus, dude, we're changing in here!" Mary yelled, her words reaching no one but me. The panda-clad intruder was already gone.

A tangle of thoughts crowded my mind. This guy had just kicked in our cabin door and had his camera on. Did I pull down my top in time? Did this dude just get footage of my boobs? Is this going on the internet?

Mary scoffed and began stretching. Our other friends arrived shortly after, and Mary told them what had happened. They all rolled their eyes and huffed "jerk." I was still processing it when the conversation moved on. I told myself not to let it bother me. I was in one of the best skate facilities in the country with friends; I shouldn't let one disrespectful asshole in a panda suit ruin that. I paid good money to be here, damn it!

I tried to tell myself it wasn't a big deal and to give him the benefit of the doubt. How was he supposed to know we were changing before he kicked his way into our cabin? But Mary and I asked other people if he busted in their cabins and they said no. And even if he didn't know we were changing, he didn't have any business kicking in our cabin door, especially not while filming.

I actually knew who the panda-suited guy was because we're both based in Columbus. I thought he was an alright guy before, though I'd never met him, because we had mutual friends and he was always posting videos of the creative places he skated around the city. Before he kicked in our door, I'd been looking forward to meeting him. Instead, for the rest of the weekend, I avoided him and unfollowed him on social media, which was clearly the opposite of what he wanted given the number of panda stickers he slapped around Woodward bearing his social media handles.

Back in Columbus, a couple of friends asked me how my second time at Woodward had been. I told them it was great—minus worrying if a nonconsensual video of my boobs was floating around the internet somewhere. By that point, I'd spent two whole days telling myself it wasn't a big deal, so I was taken aback by my friends' defense of me.

"Who the fuck does that?" one yelled.

"I'm so sorry that happened to you," another said. "That's awful."

It wasn't until I heard my friends' concern that I realized I had a right to be angry. I was in my cabin with the door closed, and he wasn't one of the people bunking in my cabin. I had a right to expect some measure of privacy, and he had violated that for the sake of a stupid video.

My friends asked if I was going to report the incident to the event organizers. I considered it, but a few things stymied me. Out of the hundreds of people at the rollerblade event, it seemed less than fifty were women. Out of the women, I was pretty sure I was the only one from Columbus. The guy was a small-time blading celebrity and had clout among his people. I worried that if I reported him, the organizers might, out of loyalty, tell him who had made the report. I could even envision his response: "I don't even know her!"

And it's true—he doesn't know me. That incident was the first and what I hoped would be the last time we ever interacted in person. But with those handful of words, I'd be rendered just another "crazy," "hysterical" woman, jealous of a man's success, deriving joy from taking him down. Regardless of how untrue it was, I knew that's how the story would get played. It always does.

So when I saw the other stupid video, the viral one of him rollerblading naked down a busy interstate, and all the comments from fellow skaters telling him how cool he was for endangering himself and the drivers on the road that day, I seethed. All that anger from when he kicked in my door boiled back to the surface.

Several local media outlets wanted to do profiles on the guy, especially after he began using the viral video as a way to launch his professional rollerblading career. He started a GoFundMe to cover any legal fees resulting from the video and to continue bringing his content to people because he likes "making viewers smile." He didn't seem to care how many people he upset during the making of the videos.

It was the media's interest that led my reporter friend to text me about the guy, but after I told him about the creepy run-in I'd had with the panda-headed fool, he killed the story. Later, another reporter asked me if I would talk to him on the record about what I had experienced. I learned there were more allegations from other female skaters about the guy's behavior. Allegations that included sexual assault.

I did a dozen mental calculations, as all women do when asked to speak about their experiences with creepy men.

If he denied it, would people believe me? If people believed me, would they care? If he found out it was me, would he sic his fans and followers on me and have me doxxed or otherwise harassed? Would it lead to me or other women getting harassed at skate parks or ousted from our skate communities? Would I be run out of skate spaces in my own city? Would people just say I was trying to keep him from being successful? Would I be cast as "the bad guy" in the footnote of his story?

After tallying the results of my calculations, I saw that there was little to nothing to be gained for me in coming forward, and I stood to lose so much more. I opted not to speak to the reporter.

Nearly five months later, the reporter reached out to me again. More women had come forward with reports of this guy being creepy. The reporter once again asked if I'd talk to him.

By this point, I had another important thing to consider: this book.

I wanted to write *Midwest Shreds* because I love skating. I love skates and the skaters who skate them. I love skate parks and the people who build them. If soulmates can be sports, then skating is mine—my soul-sport. Roller skating is my religion, skate parks are my cathedrals, and I'll genuflect with my knees bent in supplication each time I face off with a wall of curved concrete. And I didn't want speaking out about some loser in a panda head to jeopardize this book, the sport I love, or my participation in it.

It wasn't that I didn't trust the reporter to handle the story with care. He'd broken stories about sexual assault and written them with delicacy. I worried that if I talked to the reporter, no rollerbladers or other skaters in Columbus would want to be interviewed for this book. It was selfish, I admit, but it wasn't a risk I was willing to take. At least not then.

When I first moved to Columbus, Ohio, from Birmingham, Alabama, I was shocked by the kindness, compassion, and generosity present on a societal level. There are assholes everywhere, of course, but coming from a place that touts its "southern hospitality" to a place that seemed more hospitable in every sense of the word was jarring. At Kroger, a woman saw me juggling avocados, trying not to drop them, so she took them one by one from the pile on my arms and chest and put them into a bag. On that same grocery trip, I saw a coupon shoved onto the shelf next to the item it was for—some kind soul wanting to save the next person a few cents.

I saw this same kindness and generosity reflected in the skate community. From the women who welcomed me like I was their long-lost best friend and taught me all the tricks they knew, to the man who insisted on giving me some proper skateboard wheels when he saw that I'd put my roller skate wheels on my new deck, my first skateboard since the one that's probably still rotting in a storm drain in Alabama. From the skaters who plan free events for women, trans, and nonbinary folks to get more comfortable on their wheels and at skate parks to the more seasoned skaters who teach enthusiastic kids who are new to the sport. By and large, the skate community in Columbus is one of love, like the heart-shaped state the city is in the middle of. And I found this is true for all the places I visited throughout the Midwest for this book. After talking to dozens of skaters across half a dozen states, I can tell you that skaters by and large are the best people.

That doesn't mean that all skaters are good people simply because they skate. Dudes don't stop being creepy the moment they strap wheels to their feet. In the same way that football and basketball stars are propped up and worshiped for their athletic prowess in spite of the women they abuse who become collateral damage in their singular careers, however, I saw women in the skate community be lulled by this guy too.

In a group chat with upwards of ninety women and nonbinary skaters, one woman spoke up about her experience with the guy as a heads-up to the rest of us that he wasn't a safe person to be around. Another woman spoke up: *Me too.* And another. And another. I watched the texts roll in, remaining silent to give these women space and because their encounters with him were so much worse than mine. For a moment, I felt the power of the whisper network doing what it does best: trying to keep vulnerable people safe.

But that only lasted a moment because soon, another string of texts started pouring through my screen.

He's always been so nice to me.

Maybe he was just having a bad day? Every time I run into him at the skate park he always helps me with whatever trick I'm working on.

Idk, I thought he gave kids skate lessons? He seems like a good guy.

This, coming from women. This, after the #MeToo Movement was in full swing. This, after this very group text was intentionally set up as an inclusive, safe space. The whole point was that there's strength in numbers, and if female and nonbinary quad skaters coordinated times to skate together, then none of us would be alone at the skate park and we'd have a support system if guys got weird. Aghast, I fumed.

"Hey, he was creepy with me too . . ." I began, sharing what happened to me, naively believing that I wouldn't be shot down like the women before me were. Wanting to believe that there's strength in numbers here, too. Instead, the messages continued.

I just can't believe we're bashing a member of our local skate community like this.

Where's the proof?

This pile-on is making me uncomfortable.

Disgusted, hurt, and angry, I left the chat, resolving to never skate with any of them again. Even those who didn't outright rebuff me and the other women who were victims of this creep still didn't stand up for us. More than anything, there was silence in numbers, and silence is complicity. I thought about Kate, who had started the group chat, added new members, and moderated when necessary, and Jules, another one of the original handful of us local quad park skaters who was usually active in the group chat. I thought we were friends, but then I thought about their silence.

For months, I skated by myself, not telling anyone when I was going out and hoping I wouldn't run into any of them. With ninety quad skaters being on that text chain, it felt like every roller skater in town was in that group, so I resolved that I wouldn't skate with anyone on quads, at least not for a long time.

That's why I ignored the first couple of notices I saw for Community In Bowls Columbus meetups. CIB originally began in New Zealand as a way to get more women, particularly quad skaters, comfortable at skate parks. In the years since, chapters have popped up all over the world. But I figured the CIB Columbus chapter would include the same people who'd been in the group text, and I wasn't interested.

But as so many skaters do, I connected with Emilie Yguado, one of the organizers of CIB Columbus, on Instagram. She's so gregarious that she goes up to strangers at the skate park and makes a habit of introducing herself. I didn't recognize her at first—not after over a year of mask wearing—but I could soon spot her from a mile away by her orange helmet, which was painted like a jack-o-lantern, and her tattoo-covered limbs.

Still, I was nervous when I met up with her at Fairwood Skate Park in Columbus. The skate park is across town from me and not one I usually go to, and after the run-in with the creep, I'm always nervous going to new skate parks around the city where I don't know the regulars. Plus, I didn't know her well. Was she one of the roller skaters who capes for creeps and doesn't believe women? My anxiety was on edge, volleying from a kind of Schrödinger's friendship.

At the time we talked, Emilie had just had her one-year skativersary, having started a couple of months into the pandemic. She was working a stressful job as the manager at a restaurant and bar that was shut down for twelve weeks during the lockdown, and when they were able to reopen, nearly everyone but her and a handful of other people were laid off. Even before COVID hit, she was working upwards of fifty hours a week and was craving work-life balance. Enter roller skating.

"Skating helped me not be so bummed out," Emile said. "I couldn't see my friends in the pandemic, but I was still doing something fun."

Over the coming months, she started going to socially distanced skate meetups in a covered parking garage in town. Then winter hit. Skating outside was miserable at best and downright dangerous at worst. Emilie and her friend Hannah bought keyholder passes to the Cassady Bowl, a DIY in town.

"I was able to skate there, and it helped me get out of the winter funk. The Cassady Bowl is known to get a little crazy," she said, recalling skateboarders breaking beer bottles in the bottom of the bowl and setting each other's clothes on fire, then posting the videos to Instagram. "So we'd go in the morning real early, like seven o'clock. True wake and skate style. If I didn't have that bowl to go skate every morning, I probably would've been a sad depressed person getting the winter blues."

The Cassady Bowl went the way of so many DIYs due to mismanagement and lack of funds to pay rent—with a little help from ill-behaving dudes.

"There was some beef with the skateboarders over the bowl. When they posted their goodbye announcement on Instagram, I posted this sweet sentimental comment about how I made some really good friends there and good memories. I learned how to park skate and pump properly there. I learned to drop in there and I feel like my tailbone will never recover from the slams. It'll always hold a special place in my heart," Emilie said. "Then one of the dudes replied like, 'All these people saying they're going to miss the bowl should've paid rent.' And I was like, 'Yo, that's not cool because a lot of us *did* pay rent.' Then Cassady Bowl blocked me on Instagram and upgraded their goodbye event to skateboarders only for quote-unquote safety concerns. It's shitty they had to go out that way."

Around the same time, a local brewery that catered to skaters started having events where they'd set up portable skate obstacles in a parking lot. I'd considered going many times, but when I saw how many quad skaters showed up, and not wanting to immerse myself back into the community so quickly, I avoided it.

"I started hearing some things about . . . we had some concerns about some of the people that they associate themselves with," Emilie began diplomatically. "I heard those things. I was sexually assaulted when I was a child, and it took me a long fucking time to heal from that. And I remember how people tried to make it seem like I was lying."

It was him. The concerns from the community were about the panda-headed blader. And she had all the same concerns I did. I breathed a sigh of relief so loud I gasped.

"You see it too. I'm not crazy," I said. Emilie nodded.

After I left the quad skating group chat, the group continued to promote and host events at the brewery, knowing the predatory blader would be present. He was all over the brewery's Instagram page. It wasn't a secret.

"There are people who have had similar experiences with this guy and because of who he is and how popular he is, it's like people don't care. It's unfortunate," she said. "But I'd rather have someone know that I *do* care and know that I choose not to associate with him or anyone else who associates with him."

I blinked back tears, hoping Emilie wouldn't notice. It wasn't until she put it into words herself that I was able to quantify the anger I felt. I was sexually assaulted in my dorm room my freshman year of college. This space that was supposed to be a sort of home for me didn't feel safe after that and it rocked me. The guy who did it was popular on our small campus, and I worried no one would believe me. I didn't want to drop out of college—I wanted to be there, but being there required me to confront the memories of my assault every moment I spent in my dorm room. That was how it felt when the women in the quad group chat shouted down the women who raised concerns about this problematic skater in town. I didn't want to quit skating—I love it—but every time I skated with another quad skater, I couldn't help wondering if they were one of those who tried to silence the women who were brave enough to speak up. And every time I thought about it, I remembered how the situation mirrored that night in my dorm room a decade before and how full of rage I still was and probably always would be.

Skating had begun as my outlet, but in the months since the fallout from the quad group, it had turned into a socially acceptable way of beating myself up. I could take out my rage on my own body in a way that protected me from the scrutiny of those who would tell me I needed help. My self-destruction wasn't as noticeable as my past eating disorder and wasn't as deadly as the years I spent cutting in middle and high school. At the skate park, I could be angry, and my anger was productive. My anger made me skate harder and faster and let me unlock tricks I dreamed of when I could focus my mind enough to channel the fury.

But fury is a bright fuse, an accelerant that blazes hot and will incinerate you if you let it. It wasn't until I sat on the grass on the edge of Fairwood Skate Park with Emilie, the polyphonic jingle of an ice cream truck echoing through the parking lot, that I realized I was tired of being mad. I was tired of acquiring bruises like trophies with little regard for my well-being. I was tired of letting bad dudes ruin what were supposed to be enjoyable experiences and safe communities for me. I was tired of living in fear of other skaters.

The skate community is a microcosm of the world at large—there are good people and bad people, people concerned with justice and people who abuse, people who cape for those abusers, and people who stand up to them. And caught in the middle, there are people who are silenced out of fear, wondering who will believe them if they come forward.

"I flat out said, 'I know you've been told he's a creep by multiple people and you guys still keep supporting a group that's associated with him and that's not cool.' I have no interest in sitting there and being complicit with that. You can't shoot people down when they're telling you things," Emilie said. I wanted to hug her for being braver than I was, for saying what needed to be said when I couldn't.

It wasn't long after that when Emilie and Hannah started the CIB Columbus chapter. I started going to their meet-ups. I slowly folded myself back into the fabric of the skate community. I went to parks I didn't normally go to, like Fairwood, with its butter-smooth concrete, tight bowl that's perfect for fast carves, and its regulars with their blend of wheels. I have yet to run into any unsavory characters there. The kindness of nearly everyone I meet reaffirms my faith in the humanity of this community.

There was, too, the guilt I felt that part of the downfall of the original quad group was my fault. I remember when there were basically only five of us who would regularly go to Skate Naked in our roller skates and we first decided to form a skate collective with events, matching T-shirts, and a dedicated Instagram account. At the time, I was working a day job that drained me while trying to build up my freelance writing business on the side. I felt like I barely had time to skate, much less contribute meaningfully to organizing the collective, with all the time I spent working. I didn't have the bandwidth to be a leader, and by the time my life had cooled down, I didn't have the right to demand a voice in the decision-making process. In hindsight, I wish I'd stepped up more at the beginning, before decisions were made that I wasn't a part of and didn't agree with. I'm as much to blame as anybody, and I've spent more time now learning how to forgive myself than I have being encapsulated by fury at everyone else.

I chose to write about my cabin door being kicked in and my space being violated and my boobs being filmed now because I know that's not how the skate community at large is—nor is it how I believe the future of the skate community will behave as progress marches forward with time. In 2019, when the incident at Woodward happened, I was a fairly new skater, and for all I knew, that's how most skaters were—*Jackass* and *Viva La Bam* wannabe pranksters two decades out of style. Looking back, I'm glad I didn't quit skating and that I gave the community a chance to show me that guy was an outlier. But I also think about other women and other marginalized skaters who might have encountered something similar or worse and who now don't feel safe in their local skate community.

I don't think it's possible to truly love something without critiquing it or at least noticing its flaws and demanding it be better, do better. That's why my feelings about skating are complicated. I must reconcile loving a flawed thing and its flawed people.

After more than a year went by without having seen the organizers of the original quad group, I ran into Kate at Skate Naked. In spite of myself, I grinned ear to ear when I saw her. I was genuinely overjoyed. We hugged, and I felt nothing but love for her, all bitterness gone.

"I was thinking of coming here every Monday night," she said. "Like we used to."

Like we used to when there were just five of us, casually skating and hanging out. Before the collective, before the official events, before the pressure and the demands—before, even, we were any good.

"No Instagram, no T-shirts, no group chat, just skating," Kate added.

When I let my anger go, I stopped being infuriated with her. When I stopped guilting myself for what I hadn't done, I stopped blaming her for what she did do. When I forgave myself, I forgave her too.

"I'd like that," I answered, smiling. "I'd like that a lot."

CONCLUSION

In the wee hours of the morning of Thursday, June 29, 2023, I was doomscrolling on Instagram, unaware of the doom that unfolded just a few hours before. At first, I thought the photos were old pictures of Notre Dame aflame, so bright was the burning orange cathedral against the night sky. But the cathedral's tower was different, and the windows were too.

Sk8 Liborius was burning.

The grand church of skating—a pilgrimage site for the wheely inclined, a spiritual skate experience for even the staunchest of atheist and agnostic skaters, and an item on countless skaters' bucket lists—was engulfed in a four-alarm fire. No one was injured, but the skate park was destroyed; the roof collapsed and all the wooden ramps turned to ash. A simultaneous piece of architectural and skate history was lost in one fell swoop.

It was 3:00 a.m. in Ohio, and my stomach dropped. I involuntarily covered my mouth with my hand and fought a wave of panicked dread. So many skate parks crumble into disrepair or close from lack of funds, but the skate community in St. Louis and across the country fought so hard to keep that from happening to Sk8 Liborius. To see all the love and effort that had been poured into it go up in flames—even from afar—was gut-wrenching. I had a sense of mourning, like I'd lost a person, not a building.

But of course, buildings are more than structures. The most precious buildings aren't beloved because of their design, architecture, or decor. While these things are important, what really makes a place special is the community that loves it and cares for it; the people who make that place home in a literal or figurative sense. Sk8 Liborius was home to many skaters, and now it's gone.

I watched the news unfold in those early morning hours as I sat in my recliner with my leg propped up. Since breaking my right ankle the month before and having surgery that left me with a metal plate, seven screws, two "tightropes"—hardware to keep torn ligaments in place so they could heal properly—and a 5.5-inch scar, I have to elevate it to keep the swelling down. When the sun rose, the local skaters convened at Sk8 Liborius to survey the damage and saw that the walls still stood, but everything inside was ruined. I felt a kinship with the skate park—we were both broken, and while we could be repaired, we'd never be quite the same.

I broke my ankle trying to shred a bowl that ended up shredding me. Despite replaying the scene in my head a thousand times, I couldn't tell you exactly what happened. One minute I was riding the wall, and the next minute, I felt the world shift beneath me. One minute I was soaring in defiance of gravity, and the next, I was on my ass with my foot twisted under me. I heard the bone––two bones actually––snap and knew instantly it was broken.

In the weeks that followed, dozens of people asked me if I was ever going to skate again. "Hell yeah," I laughed. "That's the first thing I'm going to do when the doctor clears me for activity." For me, the question wasn't *if* I would skate again, but *when*. That part was unclear: my surgeon speculated four to six months post-operation. The answer depends on so many factors—how well and fast my bones and ligament heal, how quickly I get mobility back in physical therapy, whether I reinjure myself before I'm fully healed, etc.—that it would be impossible to say.

The same is true for Sk8 Liborius. The cathedral was already in need of major upgrades and repairs before the fire, so the burning could sound the death knell. Or it could be a wake-up call for the skate community of just how precious a place like Sk8 Liborius is, and the burning could be the impetus needed to rally the community to save it in a lasting way.

As the day progressed, more and more St. Louis skaters gathered at Sk8 Liborius in what felt like loved ones coming to the bedside of a dying relative. One posted a video of him opening the double-doored entrance—the one that welcomed people into the skate park's narthex—and a river of gray, sooty water pouring out. It came down the entrance stairs like a waterfall and overflowed the sidewalk. It was a sobering sign of just how hard the fire department had tried to save the church. Inside, the floor was sludgy with grime and ash-mud, fallen ceiling beams perched themselves at precarious angles, and the only roof was the open sky.

In one of the photos of the aftermath, you can see one of the many murals that once decorated the walls is still intact. It's a grayscale portrait of a person with long bangs brushed to the side and they're smiling wide, the gap between their teeth visible. The person appears to be looking where the choir loft once was, a look of incandescent joy wrinkling the corners of their eyes. Far above their painted head is another painting, this one from its original use as a Catholic Church: *I am the vine.*

The longer original quote comes from John 15:5: "I am the vine; you are the branches. If you remain in me and I in you, you will bear much fruit; apart from me you can do nothing." Many Christians have interpreted the verse to mean God is the tendril from which all else grows, and it's the job of his followers to branch out, spreading his message. But in the context of Sk8 Liborius, I read it another way. Skate spots, especially skate parks, are the vines from which skaters grow, and we skaters are the branches, meant to make this sport welcoming and supportive to all who wish to participate in it.

I think of the "branches" I climbed to get out of the bowl when I broke my ankle, the people who let me use their limbs as a trellis so I could get to safety. Some of them were perfect strangers. Some I'd only met a handful of times before. Two skaters held each of my hands as I hyperventilated from pain. A skater I'd never before met drove me to the emergency room because I just had to be extra and break my driving foot. When I got back home, still more skaters came to visit, bringing me everything from snacks to weed to a boot so I didn't have to buy my own. The skate community is full of branches, always ready to lift you up when you need something to hold onto.

They say when a broken bone fully heals, the broken spot is stronger and more resilient than the rest of the bone, less apt to break again in the future. At six weeks post-surgery, I believe it. Despite the shock of my surgeon and physical therapist who have said multiple times how abnormal this is for this stage in the healing process, I'm already walking with no boot and no crutches. I wear an ankle brace when I leave the house, but at home my foot is naked. They said I can skate at three months post-op, a month earlier than the earliest initial estimate I was given.

I'll take it easy my first time back, but I cannot fucking wait to skate again. Even so, I'm not the same skater I was before the break. While injuries are common in action sports, I know I'll go back more fearful than I was before, not wanting to risk further pain and fractures. I'll have to learn to trust the capabilities of my body again and relearn skills I once knew with confident muscle memory. I imagine the same is true for Sk8 Liborius. Though itself inanimate, I imagine the skaters who built its ramps, maintained the building, and raised money to keep the lights on won't be the same after the fire. Even though they announced the intention to rebuild, it won't be like it was. Like my ankle, there will be a long and lasting scar.

But if there's one thing I know about skaters, it's that we're tenacious and resilient. We don't give up. We'll fall down ten times and get back up eleven. We'll try and try again. We'll keep going. We may not be the same—we may not even necessarily be better—but we always come out stronger in the end.

There's a double meaning to "Midwest Shreds" that I didn't notice when I initially thought up the title to this book. Yes, the skaters of the Midwest do shred, but there's another element to it too. The Midwest is often given scraps, mere shreds of the respect the coasts get. Yet those of us here take those shreds and make something good out of them. Something folks out here know better than to fly over or drive through.

Take it slow, and you'll find that the scenic route is dotted with skate parks.

The Midwest is mocked because people say there's nothing here but cornfields and farmland, but the fact is that this country wouldn't be able to eat if it weren't for "flyover country." The Midwest feeds the entire country. And the rest of American skate culture needs the Midwest to feed it as well. I wouldn't have started park skating if I hadn't moved here. There wasn't enough of a skate park culture in the South (though that's changing—the fourth largest skate park in the country recently opened in Birmingham, Alabama, the same city I used to lament for having nowhere to skate), and there's so much of it out west that it's intimidating. Like a plant in its habitable zone, I needed the conditions here to thrive.

Skating at all the different parks I've written about here made me a better and more confident skater. It's easy to get stuck in a rut where you only want to skate on one particular obstacle or at the one park that feels like home. Especially if you're not as good as you want to be, you feel like you can only do certain tricks in a certain space. Making yourself go to different parks forces you to get better on new terrain and to get comfortable testing your skills in new environments. It's good for you.

Going to all these different places throughout the Midwest also made me more aware of the pervasive issues affecting the entire community. Over half the people I interviewed were frustrated by the lack of indoor skate parks and the difficulty of keeping indoor and DIY skate spaces alive. They spoke, too, about the community being cliquey and needing more diversity and how creating a welcoming atmosphere is a matter of accessibility.

So much of the beef between skaters—no matter what kind of wheels they're riding—has to do with skaters historically being pushed to the side. We're athletic, but we're not jocks. Though we no doubt have communities, we enjoy solitude to a degree, since nonteam sports are by nature self-motivated ventures. Because of that pseudo-isolation and ostracization from mainstream athletics (though perhaps not so much for skateboarders anymore now that it's an Olympic sport), skaters can easily end up replicating those same gatekeeping systems of power in their own communities. Discussions over who's a "real" skater and who's a poseur, whose wheels are better, or which group does better tricks are all forms of gatekeeping and exclusivity.

I'm not saying we need to hold hands and sing "Kumbaya" with the football team or the members of the bowling league, but there's something to be said for amicable coexistence with people who, unless they're wealthy and landed enough to build their own private skate park at their house, have to share facilities. We're all making blood sacrifices to the concrete.

The thing about skating is that there's always more to learn. There's always a new trick or a more extreme version of an old one. There's always a new place to skate, and although they may look similar, no two parks skate exactly the same. The pros of yesteryear were so much more mellow than the pros of today, just as I expect the pros of today will be mellower compared to those of the future. With the changing metrics and the constant, beautiful evolution of the sport, to ask myself when I will feel like I've reached peak authenticity as a skater is an exercise in futility. Maybe I'll never reach it. Or perhaps one day I'll be skating along and feel so comfortable in my skin, at the park, uncaring over whether or not my run is being filmed or even whether or not I nail my tricks, that I'll feel totally zen and know that yes, I am an authentic skater. And in realizing that, I'll also know that authenticity doesn't fucking matter.

This is not to say that I don't currently feel zen when skating. Skating ramps is the perfect meditation because you can't live anywhere but in the moment or you'll bust your face. It's the ideal drug, producing adrenaline and endorphins at an alarming volume. I have been too depressed to go skating, but I have never been depressed while actually skating. I am at my calmest when gliding down the inclines of a ramp, praying to a god I don't believe in not to die. Skate culture is full of contradictions.

What would make me feel authentic and zen would be to feel my skates like I feel my feet, a natural extension of my legs, something I don't have to question or think too hard about how to use. That is to say, I want skating to feel as natural as walking, even as I'm skating surfaces that are so steep and slick that even walking them would be a challenge. The ramps I most enjoy skating don't have the gentle incline of wheelchair ramps; they have a steepness that makes your stomach drop, like that moment at the top of the rollercoaster where you feel weightless for a moment before gravity pulls you down.

Perhaps I have unreasonable expectations for myself and for skating. But what is skating, especially ramp skating, if not unreasonable? There's no logical reason to do it. There's no logic to subjecting oneself to the whims of speed-generating inclines and small spinning wheels. The whole enterprise is unreasonable, and yet we do it anyway because it's fun.

One morning, after waking up sore and bruised from the previous night, when I fell and that fall was broken by my boob and I nearly passed out, I asked myself: "If I shred skate parks for the next twenty years and I never get any better than I am right now, would I still be happy?"

The biggest bowl at Skate Naked is six feet deep with a bit of vert at the top, and it haunts my dreams. I've stood on its deck countless times, willing myself to step over the coping and trust my muscle memory to carry me safely to the bottom and up the other side. I've visualized myself dropping in, and I've gone to the skate park with every intention of finally doing it, only to come away angry at myself, my body, my fear, and my risk aversion for not having done it.

I set myself a goal of besting that bowl by the time I turned in this book manuscript. With three weeks to go, I decided *today is the day, for real this time*, for the last time.

My legs shook as I stood on the deck. Why was I so afraid? This bowl was only a foot deeper and a little steeper than the mini-ramp I skate all the time. There was no logical sense to my fear. I looked straight down and said aloud to my friend Tabi, who had conquered the bowl long ago and helped pep-talk me, "It's not even that deep."

"It's not," she agreed. "I guarantee you have the skills to do this."

I let my leg hover in the air for a moment before stepping over the coping and leaning into the depths. The ground met me with a slam. Without quite being sure how it happened, I landed on my ass. But it didn't hurt! I survived! I whooped and pulled myself out of the bowl to do it again.

The second time, I felt confident enough to ask Tabi to film me. I stepped over the coping and a half-second later was reeling from the impact to my tailbone. My head throbbed, feeling as though my brain had been shaken inside my skull like a baby's rattle. I lay at the bottom of the bowl, trying to catch the breath that was knocked out of me, all the while muttering, "fuck fuck *fuckfuckfuck* . . ."

In watching the video afterward, I could see exactly what I had done wrong. I hadn't bent my knees enough, hadn't leaned far enough forward, hadn't had my feet as far apart as they should've been. I didn't stagger-bend-lean like I should have; I didn't do the basics. I assumed my body had been skating ramps long enough that if I had the will, it would find the way. I thought something inside me would know what to do. My tailbone stayed sore for days, but my pride suffered a hematoma.

Skating is amoral. It doesn't care if it's your competition day or if you've been skating for years and you "should" be able to do that trick by now. Skating doesn't give one damn about whether you're at a new, unfamiliar park or if there's someone you're trying to impress or if you really need a video clip for the 'gram. And it certainly doesn't care if you've been hyping yourself up for weeks and finally feel ready to conquer a ramp that scares you. You skate, you fall, you bruise and scratch and scrape and live to skate another day.

I ask myself again if I would be happy doing this for twenty years, never progressing, always busting my ass. The answer is yes. Unequivocally, irrevocably yes.

Sources and Resources

Several people I interviewed for this book are running skate organizations that make a difference in their communities on a shoestring budget. If you feel inspired by these stories, I hope you'll give as generously as your means will allow.

Keep Pushing: Dan Mancina's nonprofit to build the first publicly accessible skate park for blind and low-vision skaters: https://www.keeppushinginc.com/.

froSkate: A Chicago-based skate collective organized by Karlie Thornton that provides transportation and gear to queer and/or BIPOC skaters who might not otherwise have access to the city's skate facilities: https://www.froskate.com/.

Pushing Together: A nonprofit organized by Ariel Ries of Fargo Skateboarding that provides access to the skate park, gear, lessons, and other resources for children and young adults living in poverty in DeKalb, Illinois: https://pushingtogethernfp.com/.

Sk8 Liborius and the Liborius Urban Arts Space: A destination skate park and nonprofit arts center in St. Louis, Missouri: https://www.gofundme.com/f/save-sk8-liborius.

Skate Church: Skate Church in Davenport, Iowa. It accepts donations to maintain the skate park and to operate the church's food pantry: https://www.facebook.com/skatechurchdav and/or http://www.thecenter-davenport.com/skate-church-hours-and-forms.html.

BladeCLE: A rollerblading organization based in Cleveland that organizes street contests around Ohio: https://bladecle.lazyfitter.com/.

Many skaters also share their shredding on Instagram, so if you'd like to follow some of the people I interviewed for this book, you can do so at the following handles:

- @midwestshreds
- @skatenakedskatepark
- @schmidtys_ramp_and_camp
- @dogblader
- @sk8liborius
- @hoopsiedee
- @elex.us
- @slappysinclair
- @skatechurch.davenport
- @skatechurchmovement
- @dewtour
- @dsmskatepark
- @skatedsm
- @thetiapearl
- @danthemancina
- @riedellskates

- @theshredshedwi
- @tunafiche
- @natsuko.suzu
- @froskate
- @pardonmythrashing
- @royalsna
- @keemosupremo89
- @gnarlyjargon
- @fargoskateboarding
- @fargo.skatepark
- @pushingtogethernfp
- @thenew1994
- @radical.wheels
- @bipocwhoskate
- @bladecle
- @dressupjesus
- @timabaduh
- @emilieyguado
- @cibcolumbusohio
- @groovyunicyclist
- @unicycleclubosu

Acknowledgments

The trouble with acknowledgments is there are so many people who have taught, supported, and encouraged me along the way that I'll inevitably forget someone and then feel guilty about it. So consider these acknowledgments, like the rest of this book, noncomprehensive. As with many things in life, there's always more behind the scenes.

To Javacia Harris Bowser and the entirety of See Jane Write, who have encouraged me endlessly, taught me how to write and pitch, and have celebrated every win alongside me. I'm not even sure I'd be a writer without the past decade of love and education you've invested in me. Thank you.

To Dr. Weber, my English teacher at Gardendale High School, and Professor Joseph Stitt and Dr. Jane Archer at Birmingham-Southern College—you told me I had what it takes to be a professional writer. Thank you for making me want to prove you right so badly that I actually did it.

To Amanda Page, Samantha Tucker, and the many writers over the years who have generously read and critiqued my creative nonfiction, thank you. You gave me the loving kick in the ass I needed to be able to write a book.

Massive and unending thanks to every single person who let me interview them in person, via phone, and through video for this book.

Your enthusiasm and generosity of time, talent, and treasure made this book. Your names are in these pages, so I won't repeat them here and risk accidentally leaving someone out. I'm honored to know all of you. You make the Midwest skate community what it is. Thank you!

To everyone who has made my skating journey joyful, whether your name graces these pages or not, thank you. Special thanks to Tabi Mund and Kate Davis, who taught me much in my earliest days on the ramps, and to Jessica Warner, Ash Thompson, Isabel Andrews, Laurel Phaneuf, Christy Williams, Aaron Hobgood, Mase (whose real name I don't even know!), Emma Remley Heiberger, and the multitude of Columbus, Ohio, skaters who have made skating in this town so fucking fun.

To Martha Bayne, who originally acquired this book at Belt Publishing. Your excitement and enthusiasm for this idea fueled me, thank you.

To Michael Jauchen and Anne Trubek at Belt, who gave such thoughtful edits on this manuscript, thank you, thank you, thank you. It's true that every writer needs an editor, and I'm fortunate this book got two of the best in y'all.

To the rest of the team at Belt, thank you to everyone who had any hand at all in shaping this book. It takes a village.

Thank you to my sister-in-law, Katy Peper, for giving me a place to stay while I was in Minneapolis. And to my niece, Melanie: Skating with you was the highlight of my trip.

Thank you to Jane and Sid Kahan for opening your home in Detroit to me. I've always said book friends are the best friends, and Jane, you consistently prove that to me. I'm so glad you randomly found my blog all those years ago.

Thank you to Katie Roth and Mark Clark, the mom and stepdad of one of my favorite humans, who generously opened their home to me in Des Moines. I had so much fun spending time with y'all, and it's no surprise to me how Clare turned out so great. And to Clare Roth, thank you for being one of my closest friends.

There are a multitude of friends who have believed in this book even before I did. Ethan Hamm, my childhood bestie and forever ride-or-die; Sam Shepherd, my most emotionally intelligent friend and the loudest person in my cheering section; Robyn Hammontree and Carla Jean Whitley, my fellow writers and cat mamas; Jessica Furniss, who's been with me in the creative and freelance soup for so long and is a constant well from which I draw strength; and Andi Yates, a great friend and up-and-coming writer in her own right (lookout, world!). Thank you all. I couldn't ask for a better group of friends. (And to anyone I've neglected to mention here, assume ignorance and caffeine deficiency rather than malice.)

Thank you to my cats, some of whom I've had since before I started skating and some of whom were adopted since. You can't read this, but you've been my constant companions and my happiest distractions. *Meow* *slow blink.* I hope I pronounced "thank you" right in Cat.

Last but far from least, to my ex-husband-in-progress and friend, Jon Reed: This book wouldn't exist without you. From the start, you've been nothing but supportive of my skating, even when it's kept me out late at night, taken me out of town for days and weeks on end, and when it's cut into my time with you. You've provided me with the health insurance I need to feel safe doing an action sport in my thirties and which I've certainly used. Remember that time I fell so hard on my elbow that the muscles in my bicep separated from the bone and I couldn't lift my arm without screaming for two weeks? Yeah, I try not to think about it either. You've massaged my shoulders and back when I've fallen and told me how gnarly my bruises looked, which made me feel like a badass even when I wanted to cry because hematomas are fucking painful. Thank you for introducing me to Belt back when it first launched in 2014, when we were still living in Alabama and had no idea we'd move to your hometown in Columbus—you've been instilling an appreciation for midwestern literature in me since we met. Most of all, thank you for encouraging me to write this book so often for months on end that I finally listened and started thinking it was a good idea. I remember telling you at first, "I don't have anything to say about skating," which is hilarious to me now, then, "Okay, *fine*, I'll write *one* essay," just to get you to shut up about it. Thank you for not shutting up about it.

And to anyone I've forgotten, let me know and I'll buy you a beer.

About the Author

Mandy Shunnarah is a Southern-born, Midwest-loving journalist, essayist, poet, and roller-skating enthusiast who calls Columbus, Ohio, home. Their work has been featured in the *New York Times*, *Electric Literature*, the *Rumpus*, and more. *Midwest Shreds: Skating Through America's Heartland* is their first book. Read more on their website, mandyshunnarah.com.